THE SPECTRUM

Glimpses of the Paranormal
and Encounters with the Strange

Justin Bamforth

NORMAL + PARANORMAL

The Spectrum: Glimpses of the Paranormal and Encounters with the Strange
by Justin Bamforth published by Normal Paranormal.

www.NormalParanormal.org
www.JustinBamforth.com

© 2018 Justin Bamforth

All rights reserved. No portion of this book may be reproduced in any form without permission from the author, except as permitted by U.S. copyright law.

For information contact:
info@normalparanormal.org

Book, page layout, and cover design by Justin Bamforth.
Edited by Jamie Victor, Kayshin Chan, and Carolyn Iglesias.

Revised First Edition, March 2019

ISBN 978-1-7326540-0-6

NORMAL+PAR⦀N□RM☆L

Acknowledgements

To those that have supported me throughout this ongoing adventure, I thank you for your continued patience and tolerance in listening to me ramble. My humble apologies if I went too far with this stuff back then. It's now time for me to frighten everybody else...

To Rachael Lu, Jamie Victor, Nicholas Loran, Timothy Schmidt, Kevin Valachovic, John-Michael Occhipinti, Rosalyn & Michael Lewis, Christopher Di Cesare, Alan Lewis, Marcia Moore, Marti Haines, Tina Fleming, Dan Webster, Stephanie Lewis, Rita Lin, Kimberly Yocum, Marie Gilbert, Karen Timper, Gary Sudbrink, Mandy Homer, Peter Psomiadis, Victoria Psomiadis, Traci Bachmann, Garrick Pass, Dan D. Doty, Kathy Tsai-Peng, Sharon Ho, J-Niko Chen, Christy Lu, Nehal Ahmed, Joel Kilborn, Jane Jo, Ann & Tom Coyne, Jason Jobes, Steve McLerran, Julia Jiang, Sally Zhou, Shane Sovar, Gudden Nayak, Marsha Barnhart, Marie D. Jones, and Derrel Sims—thank you all for your help and encouragement in completing this chapter of my life.

Special thanks to my three literary angels, Jamie Victor, Kayshin Chan, and Carolyn Iglesias, the first eyes on all of my projects. You help me to become a better storyteller in every aspect.

To my mother, who first turned me on to Art Bell's late-night radio program when I was younger—you taught me to look beyond circumstances, enjoy what we have, and never give up. To my father, who supported me in all my varied interests—thank you for being my tireless fan. To Carrie, for putting up with the high strangeness for well over a decade, even though it was stressful enough to simply deal with one man's weirdness.

And to my brother Sean, who pushes me to keep moving forward in life, even when I don't want to. Although we may not see eye to eye on every subject, you continually challenge me to keep asking the question, instead of being so preoccupied with the answer.

Although this book may not provide any definitive answers for what you (the reader) may seek, I hope that it encourages you to keep asking the bigger questions too.

That which is—is rarely what it seems.

Justin Bamforth
August 9, 2018

Contents

A Remedy for Headaches

Common logic leads us to believe that definitive answers are the end all be all. If we cannot uncover the underlying reason behind something, it tends to motivate us to pursue the answer even more. On the contrary, we can also just throw up our hands and exclaim, "It is what it is!" (A statement of complacency that I generally despise altogether.)

After being involved for quite some time in this obscure field of the paranormal... the supernatural... the metaphysical... or whatever you want to call it... I have finally begun to realize that pursuing definitive answers only leads to further questions. Such is the nature of this very unconventional phenomenon.

Regardless of a person's intention coming into this subject—whether it's to prove or disprove, entertain or solve—a few things are still quite evident. It's unpredictable. It's mysterious. It's so downright strange! No wonder it causes those from the believing to the doubting, a genuine headache.

People ask me if I believe in ghosts yet are surprised to hear that I don't. How can I? I don't even know what a "ghost" is to ever make the conviction that I believe in them. There is no doubt something taking place in the human experience, but it is something that is not explained by conventional means, or even verified by traditional scientific methods.

It could be the lingering spirits of deceased individuals, or what we tend to think of as ghosts.

Or...

It could be the residual effects that result from intense physical, mental or emotional energy.

Or…

It could be the subconscious manifestation of our own psychic impressions upon the environment around us.

Or…

It could be future or former selves coexisting in a parallel dimension.

Or…

It could be demons. It could be angels. It could be aliens. It could be all of the above and more.

As any researcher or investigator can tell you, what we think this is or what that isn't is merely just speculation and theories. But what it really boils down to is that we haven't a clue. Ufologists, parapsychologists, cryptozoologists, and psychic types love to neatly package the elements of the phenomena into nicely wrapped boxes of categorical descriptions. But by doing so, they overlook the possibility that it could all be related in some overarching way and yet unique in our personal perception of it.

Even though it seems to be emanating from one "place"—whether physical, multidimensional, subconscious, or something else entirely—it can take on wildly different shapes, sizes, and forms to fit the perceptions and stereotypes reflective in our thinking and beliefs. This is what I have begun to identify as the spectrum.

The ever-growing popularity with the various topics tied into the spectrum has enabled more people to talk freely about it, which is certainly a good thing. However, just because there's more investigators running around out there doesn't mean we're any closer to the groundbreaking discoveries or pioneering concepts that could bring this into the spotlight once and for all. The latest, greatest gadgets you see people using in order to prove or disprove the phenomenon certainly does not mean it's understood any better. Tools only help point people to what is and isn't working in the never-ending pursuit of its elusive nature.

What it still boils down to is further experimentation. Not just in our investigating, but also in our thinking.

I'm not a scientist, nor a psychologist, nor really even a so-called expert in this field. I am just a writer and a researcher into the curious claims of a phenomenon that seemingly goes out of its way to find me, despite how often I try to hide from it. Take the text you are about to read with a skeptical, yet open mind and formulate your own opinions. Do your own research. Use this as a starting point if you're intrigued by the topics brought about here. But always question what you think you have already come to understand. You'll spare yourself some gray hair in the process.

The thing about this study is that once we believe we've got it all figured out, some other event takes place to make us second-guess the whole damn thing. A college instructor once told me, "There are guidelines, but no rules." Of course, he was speaking about design principles, but little did he know that that piece of sound advice would come in handy in this realm too.

Noted UFO investigator Richard Lang alluded to the same concept, noting that the phenomena changes one's perception of reality.[1] We cannot go into this field with a clean approach of pure data collection. We have to tackle the subject outside our own realm of instinctual thinking and approach it how it exists—from a supernatural spectrum where anything is possible, and not merely from our own limited, three-dimensional understanding.

I am not here to convince you of the existence of bizarre phenomena, nor to deter you from any personal convictions. Some of you may have already formed logic that works out just fine based upon your own experiences, upbringing, or even spiritual background. What I strive to do here is share some of the stories I've collected, events I've experienced, and lessons I've learned so that you might gain a better sense of clarity, or comfort, knowing that you, yourself are not crazy.

We're both crazy.

---

1 Lang, Richard. "UFO Investigation and the Methodology for a New Age." Main Line MUFON Monthly Speaker Series. Tredyffrin Library, Wayne. 11 Nov. 2014. Lecture.

"There are more things that occur than we know about in this world. And so, I tend not to reject things, just listen."[2]

– Art Bell

2 *Coast to Coast AM.* Premiere Radio Networks, 08 Aug. 1997.

Encounters from an Early Age

Over the years, I've had some strange experiences, either by myself, or with others, which left me completely baffled. Even though I've wanted to investigate the events further, a lot of times that option to follow up or formally document such an experience is not readily available. Usually an experience within the spectrum is fleeting. Yet if you're fortunate to be in the right place at the right time, you're even more privileged should you get to witness the entire experience, and not just a mere glimpse of it.

In the era where modern technology is seemingly fused to our hands at every moment of every day, we tend to jump right to, "Well, where's the evidence?" After all, extraordinary claims require extraordinary evidence. But when the evidence is presented, it either falls short of our expectations because it's not good enough, or it's too good and therefore immediately discounted or regarded as a fake.

What we also fail to consider is just how awesome the experience itself can be. It can leave those not expecting it paralyzed with fear, awe or confusion. As human beings with strong reactions and emotions, we are better prepared to process an event when we are ready for it, as opposed to being taken completely by surprise.

For example, a stranger jumps out from a dark alley and scares the wits out of someone. Is that person's initial instinct to take a picture of the shadowy offender, uncertain of what their intentions could be, or is their first move motivated by the fight-or-flight response? The same could be said of a predatory creature that comes across a group of hikers in the woods. Is the first inclination an attempt to document the experience or focus on self-preservation? Maybe the need to digitally document every aspect of our lives is a high priority in this digital age, but only when we plan to do so. With a potential criminal or wild animal, we generally know what to expect, but with a presence devoid of a clear agenda or motive it takes on another aspect.

Let's say an unknown aerial object is in your presence, perhaps a mile wide that glides silently overhead and shuts down your vehicle's engine, rendering you incapable of escape. Is documenting the experience of utmost importance in that moment? Or are you left processing, perhaps even questioning everything you thought you knew about life, the universe, even God, in such a brief moment before the object takes off in the blink of an eye and your vehicle starts back up again?

Or perhaps you come home one day by yourself to witness an invisible force that tosses dishes and chairs at your head while a menacing voice emanates from every corner of the room. Is your instinct to look for a camera or to make sure you don't get physically injured instead?

Skeptics and believers alike often forget the human response to these experiences, especially in those who are not as accustomed to or as interested in the topic to begin with. But what is causing all this seemingly random craziness to occur in our lives? From extraordinary trans-dimensional encounters to more common synchronistic moments—can this all be pinpointed to a specific source with a similar agenda? It's possible there is such a rabbit hole or several of them. But the further down it we venture, the stranger the mystery becomes. To filter through and organize all this madness into some sort of cohesive form is no easy task. However, I've found that comparing reports from different case studies is especially helpful in recognizing commonalities, patterns, or traits to help identify aspects in how the spectrum of paranormal phenomena operates.

It is certainly possible that by the time you finish reading this book, the information contained within it could be archaic. But if we stay open to the possibilities of anything and everything and approach the phenomena outside of our own three-dimensional rule book, we might be able to advance in our understanding of it. Yet our understanding is also dependent on the forces operating within it, should it ever want us to understand its true nature at all. We seem to be adhering to the rules of the spectrum most of the time, as it always remains a step or two ahead of us.

As for the accounts you're about to read, I'm not looking to make or break the case for the existence of these forces. I'm passing on what I've come across in the hopes that others might be able to learn, relate, or simply share what they've experienced too. There are plenty of others waiting for the right time to tell their stories, so perhaps this book might encourage them to do so. In fact, with some of these reports, the people I spoke with were waiting for the right time as well. It took a lot of trust building and convincing in order to get them to come forward and do it. Some of them have still chosen to remain anonymous under various pseudonyms as a compromise, though I hope one day, they'll be courageous enough to come forward and reveal more.

Even if you don't believe a word of it, then at least you have something to keep the party alive with on Halloween. Just pardon the pun; my comedy act is about as good as dead.

A Flawed Recollection

I spent most of my childhood and early adolescence in the Pennsylvania town of Souderton, nestled within Montgomery County. The area is considered a suburb of Philly, yet far enough from city life to also be considered rural, in a sense. Given the number of farmlands, cornfields and the occasional waft of manure emanating in the summer air from the neighboring towns, one could argue it has the best (or worst) of both worlds. Souderton was, and still is, a popular area for raising children, as the school system is one of the best in the region. Its nearest neighbor, Telford, stands right alongside it to form one big residential supercenter.

Growing up, I developed a fascination with subjects like ghosts, UFOs and monsters (or cryptids, as they are also known as), but I didn't know about topics like negative hauntings, psychic attacks, thought-forms or generational curses. Looking back on my situation as an adult, I can now understand why certain things may have happened in the way that they did within the home I grew up in. Sometimes it's not the property that is haunted, but rather the people.

I lived in a three-story stone house along with my mother, father, and younger brother on Hillside Avenue. It was a beautiful house, but not without an array of supernatural occurrences attached to it too. Things such as phantom smells, ominous presences, movement from unoccupied floors, hat-wearing shadow figures, and even demonic faces which appeared and hovered over beds.

I think that whatever strangeness had taken place on the property, it was perhaps perpetuated by my parents' unraveling marriage. If something negative existed in the house prior to us living there, it certainly would've been fueled by enough darkness to manufacture and manifest itself into the series of troubling events we witnessed.

Sometimes my family experienced things together, and at other times, independently of one another. It's interesting to interview each of them now to observe how drastically different the recollections are. As I've interviewed others about their earliest memories of the paranormal, especially when they were children, I have begun to recognize that the memories we thought we had are not as reliable as we hope they might be. More disturbing still is that this faulty human memory of ours has the power to imprison one another as a result of supposedly accurate eyewitness testimony.

Our memories can be easily confabulated, as researcher David Jacobs, PhD. describes in his research, more specifically in regard to initial recollections of alien abductees.[3] As much as we hate to admit it, humans tend to believe their own lies or misidentifications thanks to the brain's very faulty memory recollection engine.

Psychologists define confabulation as a memory disturbance, brought about by misinterpreted, distorted or fabricated recollections without the intention to deceive.[4] This in turn creates an acceptance of inaccurate or falsified memories—or in other words, believing a lie to be truth.

In talking with those about their own childhood occurrences, the potential for confabulation greatly increases, especially given how young minds are so impressionable. It could turn out that these earliest memories are nothing more than figments of our wishful imagination, even though we swear they really happened.

According to an article published by Kerri L. Pickel in Memory, there have been numerous studies that have shown this to be true. It also becomes much more likely if the memory of an imagined event contains sensory details and/or spatial, temporal and affective information. A person might even believe that he or she actually experienced the event! If children are

---

3 Jacobs, David M., PhD. "Abductees and Their Testimony—Hypnosis and Evidence." *Walking Among Us: The Alien Plan to Control Humanity.* Kindle ed., Disinformation Books-Red Wheel/Weiser, 2015. pp. 4-5.

4 Pedersen, Traci. "Confabulation." *Psych Central,* 16 Oct. 2017. Web. 21 Oct. 2017. https://psychcentral.com/encyclopedia/confabulation/

required to visualize an event repeatedly, this form of confabulation is also quite apparent.[5]

This is why it's important to record the experience as soon as it occurs or look for corroborating testimony from others to validate the details of the event. The things we recall most vividly are the most traumatic experiences or the ones that have left their deepest impressions. But with the insignificant aspects of an experience, we tend to fill in the memory gaps with what we hope connects the story together, even though it may not have really happened that way.

A good friend of mine recalls one such event that took place when he was only five, which has stuck with him forever.[6] A dark, shadowy figure had entered the back door of his family's home, travelled through the kitchen, the living room, and out again through the front door of his house and into the house across the street. He can distinctly recall how the shadow figure floated down the steps leading to the neighbor and then immediately into it. About an hour or so later, that neighbor was found dead inside.

We usually hear reports of so-called angelic beings stepping in during life-critical situations, but there have also been darker forces witnessed in times of tragedy too. Whatever it was that my friend observed he may never know for sure, but it's certainly these types of moments that resonate with a person long after such an event has passed.

However, the equally disturbing notion is that according to his mother, the whole thing never happened in the way my friend believes it to be.[7] The event is actually something that happened to his grandmother. It turns out the grandmother had told him this story as a child, yet somehow, he adopted the event into his own memory as having actually lived it.

You can imagine the reaction when I revealed this startling conclusion to him. But I do not doubt that something remarkable must have occurred as he sticks to the strong conviction that it truly did occur to him. So maybe it did. Or maybe it didn't. Or could it have happened to both him and his grandmother?

---

5 Pickel, Kerri L. "When a lie becomes the truth: The effects of self-generated misinformation on eyewitness memory." *Memory 12.1 (2004)*: 14-26. Print.

6 JM. Personal and email interviews. 20 Mar. 2015.

7 JM's mother. Telephone interview. 25 Mar. 2015.

"We shall not cease from exploration
And the end of all our exploring
Will be to arrive where we started
And know the place for the first time."[8]

– T. S. Eliot

8 Eliot, T. S. "Little Gidding." *Four Quartets.* Houghton Mifflin Harcourt Publishing Company, 1943, 1971.

An Ongoing Education in Strange Phenomena

One of the more mind-boggling mysteries of the human experience is the doppelgänger phenomenon. To most, it implies someone that looks like them, but isn't them. The concept originates from the German definition, *double-goer*, yet in some belief systems, to encounter one's own doppelgänger is regarded as a bad omen, which leads to imminent death. Even though the doppelgänger phenomenon is seldom reported, the few instances that I have heard about never cease to amaze me.

Such is one case report from The Atlantic Paranormal Society (TAPS) in Rhode Island. Although the TAPS founders, Jason Hawes and Grant Wilson, are better known from the more popular Syfy TV show *Ghost Hunters,* some of their earlier unaired reports have implications far beyond what little we seem to understand of the ghostly realm.

In 2001, there was a case that involved George Clendennon and his wife Deborah (although those may or may not be their real names).[9] George was frustrated and perplexed by frequent conversations he would have with his wife, which she would seem to forget or even deny having. To make sure he wasn't losing his mind, George wrote down what he had told her along with the dates and times he had said it, which Deborah would still deny. George then began to catch glimpses of a female figure, which resembled his wife. But the figure would vanish into the next room

---

9 Hawes, Jason, et al. *Seeking Spirits: The Lost Cases of The Atlantic Paranormal Society.* Pocket Books-Simon & Schuster, 2009. pp. 149-150.

whenever he tried to follow her. The TAPS team was eventually contacted and brought in to look at it from another angle.[10]

When Hawes and Wilson interviewed the couple, they realized that in some instances, they weren't speaking with the real Deborah, but rather a "ghost Deborah," which functioned exactly like her real-life counterpart, but operated completely independent of her. This doppelgänger phenomenon continued throughout their investigation, so they decided to invite both women into the same room at the same time. The doppelgänger Deborah generally refused to adhere to any requests of a physical nature, such as providing a cup of water when politely asked or signing paperwork necessary to their investigation. It also refrained from speaking with them for any longer than thirty seconds before it suddenly came up with an excuse to leave. These indicators helped Hawes and Wilson to identify the real from the doppelgänger when attempting their tactic of getting both to meet. However, the doppelgänger seemed to have an acute awareness of what Hawes and Wilson were trying to do and quickly fled the scene whenever the real Deborah was within proximity to it. Eventually, with enough attempts utilizing this technique all further activity ceased.[11]

Personally, I've never had a first-hand encounter with a doppelgänger, but certain individuals that know me pretty well apparently have.

My High School Body Double

Throughout high school, I would spend lots of time at the library, primarily to use the computers there and teach myself web design or saturate myself into the world of the unexplained. My so-called doppelgänger worked at a fast food chain back in high school, or so the school librarian thought. She confronted me about it when I came in one morning.

"Thanks for taking my order last night," she said to me one day. I looked at her strangely and she seemed to pick up on my confusion. "At Wendy's, silly. You took my order."

"But, I don't work there," I replied. "I don't even have my license yet."

10 Hawes, Jason, et al. *Seeking Spirits: The Lost Cases of The Atlantic Paranormal Society.* Pocket Books-Simon & Schuster, 2009. pp. 150-151.

11 Hawes, Jason, et al. *Seeking Spirits: The Lost Cases of The Atlantic Paranormal Society.* Pocket Books-Simon & Schuster, 2009. pp. 151-154.

The fast-food restaurant she had been referring to was located a few towns over, so the only way I would have been there was if I had driven there.

"You mean you don't work at the Wendy's in Quakertown? I swear you were there. In fact, I know you work there. You have to."

I assured her that I didn't, but she was confused.

"You're messing with me, right? I mean, the person I interacted with spoke and looked just like you are speaking and standing right before me!"

I remember the conversation going on for quite some time and after many attempts of reassuring her of my real identity, I couldn't help but wonder if maybe there was really something to this whole thing, or if it was merely a case of mistaken identity. My younger brother, Sean, holds a degree in philosophy from Temple University. One of his professors at the time mentioned a theory to him, which suggested that over time, as we see and meet more people in our travels, strangers begin looking similar to those we already know. Sort of like an acute opposite to amnesia.

Over time, I've seen plenty of body doubles of my brother walking around, including some in other countries too. Once, I remember sitting across from a guy on a train that looked exactly like him from a side profile. I even took a picture of the guy and sent it to Sean to creep him out.

Could there be something to this theory? I wouldn't doubt it. But what about when two strangers recognize each other, yet can't place from where or how they know each other in the first place?

The Familiarity Fiasco

There was a rather strange encounter that occurred to me in 2002 when I resided in the small town of Landisville, Pennsylvania, located in Amish country twenty miles from the art school I attended in York. There was a Blockbuster Video in the neighboring town of Centerville that I frequented, which is where the following experience took place.

I entered the video store and noticed a much younger boy, maybe 12 or 13, who was there presumably with his sister and mother. I didn't take note of the other customers in the store at that time, just these three individuals, which I thought was a little odd in itself. The boy looked very familiar, yet I couldn't place where I had seen him before. I kept thinking it had something to do with Sean who was around the same age the boy would've been—was this kid on his soccer team or Boy Scout patrol? I approached the boy and said outright— "You look really familiar," trying not to seem like a weirdo.

Much to my surprise, he replied, "I was actually thinking the same thing about you!"

Now we both seemed like weirdos. But we couldn't place where we had met before. And I could tell it puzzled him just as much as it had with me. I offered up various suggestions as to where and how, but none of them rang a bell with him. I provided my brother's name as well as my full last name in an attempt to jog some sort of memory, yet it was to no avail.

To make matters even weirder, his slightly older sister came over and exclaimed that I looked familiar to *her*! It quickly became like a bizarre movie scene that all three of us experienced in the video store. The mom was already outside by that time and signaled to her kids to join her. Before they all left, I gave them my address on the off chance they ever suddenly remembered how we all knew each other.

But I never heard from nor saw them ever again.

Another disturbing incident took place around the same time and has to this day left me wondering about apparent body doubles and familiarity, and the amnesiac-like response mechanism that also seems to trail close behind.

Voicemails from the Subconscious

Whether our friendship began in first-grade or kindergarten is a great mystery between us, but I've known Joel Kilborn for a number of years. We've remained close throughout our lives and have spent decades concocting numerous ideas and adventures that are never truly finished. Starting several projects yet not completing most of them is the curse of creative minds it seems. But regardless, we certainly have fun enjoying the process and our time together throughout it.

Like my brother, Joel went to Temple, but to study film at its satellite campus in Ambler. He lived on campus, so I only ever visited him in the dorms a few times. Since I was two hours away out in the pastures of Lancaster County, we didn't get the chance to hang out as much as we'd liked, but we remained in close contact throughout college via instant messaging and a humor website we created and maintained. Since we were both taught web design in high school, we collaborated on a custom-built website as a way to continue our artistic efforts and poke fun at the world, our friends, and each other. It kept us out of trouble and focused creatively as young artists and writers trying to make a name for ourselves.

Joel adopted the habit of calling me "B" because of my last name. In addition to nicknames, we were familiar with each other's tendencies, quirks, flaws and traits. Most importantly was the familiarity in our voices whenever we spoke over the phone. We used the phones a lot back then to keep in touch, long before the days of text messages. However, when Joel called me up one day to presumably return my call, I was surprised. Especially when I learned that he had been returning the message I had left for him on his answering machine. But I had not called him to begin with, nor in quite some time.

"Yeah, B, you left a message on my answering machine," he assured me. "You didn't state your name or number, but I figured it was you, simply by the way you sounded. It was clearly your voice." That intrigued me, so I took it as a sign, or at least a novel attempt to get me to come down and visit him in the dorms that weekend.

Once I was there, he played me the message from his answering machine—

"Hi Joel, it's me. Give me a call back."

No name, no number, just the voice—my voice. And I certainly recognized it as mine too. I had attempted numerous musical projects in the past, so I was accustomed to hearing my own voice. But hearing one's own voice when it just should not be there is disturbing enough. Most would feel more comfortable simply trying to forget such an event had even taken place really, but somehow, I couldn't. Stranger still, Joel can barely even recall the event; let alone his entire college experience whatsoever for some equally bizarre reason.

Had I known that several years later I would actually be writing about these strange sequences, I'm sure Joel would've found reason to transfer the recording to me as a supernatural souvenir. But for whatever reason, in that moment I remember telling him to simply erase it and forget it. Perhaps I was too troubled by this possibility of another me, especially after the events that had transpired previously in high school and at the video store.

Sometimes the incidents with the paranormal leave us more disturbed than intrigued. Others believe that the unknown is best left alone for that reason. I disagree and question why I never acquired a copy of Joel's answering machine message to begin with. My usual tendencies would've compelled me to do so. But that unnatural response to the phenomenon could be one such example of the subtle manipulation these paranormal forces display in the paranormal experience as a whole. We often overlook these responses because they are so subtle. Further on in this book are some additional examples to suggest this possibility.

Casper and the Not-So-Friendly Ghost

Back in the uneventful town of Landisville, I lived in an older three-story house with two women who were aunt and cousin to Carrie—a woman I dated throughout high school and most of college. Also living in the house were a Dachshund, a Rottweiler, and an adorable black cat named Casper, whom I would later adopt and take in as my own. For a brief period, there was also a pit bull on the property, but it didn't last long due to its aggressive tendencies towards men in general. But more troubling was the unseen presence that would also show up from time to time and exhibit mischievous tendencies directed at me for whatever reason.

One particular event took place soon after I relocated from the smaller second floor bedroom to a larger converted space in the third-floor attic. The one request from Carrie's aunt was that I keep the door shut to the stairwell leading up there in order to minimize heat from escaping in the winter. Between the stairwell and my room was an uninsulated space that was partly used as storage, along with Casper's litter area.

The room was a fantastic studio space for a college kid to occupy, although that outer storage area quickly became quite extreme during the winter and summer months. So, I made sure to keep the door to the room closed along with the one at the bottom of the stairwell to satisfy the homeowner's request. Due to the age of the house, the doorframe to the room had become warped, which kept that door from being shut completely. But at the bottom of the stairwell, that door shut very tight and securely with no problems at all.

On occasion when I was in my room, I'd hear the downstairs door open by itself. Usually this occurred when I was the only one in the entire house. I thought maybe there was some burst of air that came rushing down the stairs and forced it open, or perhaps I just hadn't shut it all the way as tight as I had thought. Whatever the reason, I didn't think much of it at the time and just simply closed it again. But sometimes after coming back from school I'd be reprimanded about it even though I was certain that I shut the door perfectly tight before I left for class in the morning.

Casper learned quickly that my space acted as a sanctuary from the dogs that remained on the lower two floors of the house. He was a smart cat who could open up cabinet doors by wedging his paw underneath and pulling, but he couldn't use that technique with the attic door in the way it was constructed to the base of the stairwell. Nor could he turn doorknobs. But I went a step further to put an end to any and all possibilities of him as the culprit and installed a simple slide lock from the inside part of the stairwell. That way if I was in my room, no one would be able to open the door without first unlatching the lock from the inside. This worked for a number of nights and provided an additional level of security from outside intruders when Casper and I were the only ones in the house on occasion.

However, one morning when Carrie's aunt was home, I awoke to find the door wide open. I was completely baffled. There was absolutely no logical way it was possible. The lock had not been ripped off, but I was ripped into something fierce. I showed Carrie's aunt the extra precaution I had taken with the lock as part of my defense. At that moment, I could tell she was just as concerned as I had been.

As I was running out of options, I considered the possibility that something paranormal might have been the source. Just in case, I decided to let whatever unseen presence was there know how I felt. In a loud, stern voice I instructed it to get out since it wasn't welcome in my home and had no right to get me in trouble. It seemed that my out-loud appeal had an effect since the door never opened on its own again after that. But displaying outward hostility towards something I couldn't even accurately identify may not have been the best option. As I'd later realize, my aggressive energy could have fueled (or summoned) this unseen presence to become more aggressive with me.

A few nights after the incident, Carrie came over to visit me. There was no one else in the house but the animals and us. She was alone in the attic room reading a book when I entered quickly in a panic. I explained that when I was in the kitchen I suddenly became overwhelmed with an unsettling notion that something was upset with me. Could it have been the presence in the attic from before or something else from an investigation I went on prior? At that time, I frequented a lot of active haunted locations, but wasn't aware that these entities could follow people home and linger on afterwards.

In the moment all I knew was that some presence was aware of me and wasn't too happy with me, either. And it was on its way after me. In a terrifying moment of anticipation Carrie and I sat huddled together on the bed, with all the lights on in the room and the stereo system set to an audible level to break the eerie silence as we waited for whatever was to come in.

And then it entered—a wispy, black mass, which first passed by the stereo and increased the volume for a brief moment to startle us. We were too paralyzed with fear to move so we began repeating the Lord's Prayer. Carrie remembers a miasma of negativity with a horrible, oppressive sense of fear and pressure.[12] She also described it as something dark that was both threatening and evil as it inched closer towards us that night. Although she doesn't recall exactly how it left the room, I remember seeing the mass dissipate through the closed window. Either way, the feeling stopped rather abruptly and was presumably gone.

The experience was a valuable lesson in the powerful effect that negative energy might have in giving these things something to hold onto and manifest with. It's speculation on my part, but it's certainly one of those experiences that left its impact on the two of us. The following day Carrie presented me with a cross from the Christian bookstore she worked for as a powerful reminder of the more positive forces that can overcome the negative. I hung it above the entrance to the attic room and I never encountered another incident there.

Today, the cross remains above my current bedroom doorway as a valuable reminder of that principle.

---

12 Lindsay, Carrie. Phone interview. 24 July 2017.

"It's interesting that we know more about the distant cosmos through telescopes and cosmology, than we know about the thing that is most central to us, which is our own experiences; our own awareness—the nature of our minds."[13]

– Adam M. Curry

13 *Midnight in the Desert.* Dark Matter Digital Network / Roland Network Communications, 28 May 2018.

What I Thought I Knew

When it comes to ghostly phenomenon within the spectrum, I can't help but think that there's another angle to it. One that doesn't involve spirits whatsoever, but rather another plane of existence. And for whatever reason that alternate reality creeps into or blends in with our own more often than we realize. It can at certain times, show us or tell us of something that has been...or is yet to come.

Of course, it could also exist merely to challenge us about ever fitting any understanding of the phenomena into a neatly packaged container of logic. After all, most of what we perceive of the spectrum never makes any sense, really.

So, we'd be naive to limit ourselves to this preconceived notion of what most classify a ghost as—the spiritual energy of once living, but now deceased beings. Now consider the possibility that these "ghosts" could also be us in another form, or in another time, beyond our realm of understanding, but within our realm of existing.

We'll come back to this concept later on, but for the time being I'll share some events that have forced me to think twice about what I thought I knew...

And what I thought I'd ever experience.

The Grocery Store Time Loop

In June of 2007, Carrie and I eventually moved in together and relocated back to the Philly area. We got engaged shortly thereafter. I took a job in the affluent suburb of Bensalem, which in comparison to the low-cost of Amish country was as shocking as seeing a ghost. Prices at the grocery stores were much higher than we were used to. Now we understood why our parents, who lived in the region, had always purchased generic brands when we were growing up.

Thankfully, we found a Giant brand supermarket in town that was reasonably priced, so we quickly made that our number one go-to. But strangeness soon met us right from the beginning with the presence of a small, thin balding man who we swear we had seen at the Giant near Landisville. At the time we found it amusing but didn't think much of it. His distinct physical characteristics made him easily recognizable, even though we had hardly ever interacted with him in our old town. But that wasn't the strangest case of familiarity that occurred there.

One evening on the way home from the new job, I popped into the Giant supermarket for some groceries. As I headed down the last aisle of the store—the dairy and bread aisle—I passed by a couple coming from the opposite direction. They were an average looking couple and nothing particularly out of the ordinary struck me. But the expression they gave me certainly suggested that they knew me from somewhere. Or perhaps they knew something about me. As far as I knew, I had never seen the people before in my life.

Since I had just moved to the area, I barely knew anyone apart from those I had recently met at work. Out of courtesy, I acknowledged their presence with a friendly smile. But in the back of my mind, I wondered—had I seen them before or had they seen me somewhere else and I just wasn't aware of it? Perhaps I was the one that looked peculiar to them. Then again, I'm sure a lot of people find me peculiar in one way or another. Maybe I just simply resembled someone they actually knew.

Thinking nothing more of it, I rounded the corner to the neighboring aisle—the frozen foods section, which I usually save until the end, so those items don't melt. But I had forgotten to pick up a loaf of bread from the previous aisle. Perhaps I was too distracted with the couple that passed by earlier. I hustled down the remainder of the frozen aisle without acquiring anything, rounded the corner back to the bread and…

Sure enough, what had transpired mere moments before—the exact same couple, in the exact same placement, in the exact same manner—passed by me with the exact same expression of "knowing."

At that point, I instantly became aware that the reason they were smiling, was not because they knew me, but because they knew of this moment and the time loop that was playing itself out again. Had they been aware of it from the beginning? Had they somehow caused it?

My mind did backflips over all of the aisles in the store after that. I couldn't care less about bread or frozen whatever. I flipped around to see them almost at the end of the bread aisle with their backs turned towards me but turning the corner in the direction of where I had just been. So, I hurried back down the adjacent aisle before they did in the hopes of encountering them a third time and get to the bottom of this lunacy.

But as I bolted down that frozen aisle expecting to see the couple pop out from around the corner as their natural course should dictate, they never reappeared. *Maybe they were stuck at the bread aisle again?*

I went back down that aisle—nothing. I went back up the frozen food aisle—nothing. Had they vanished? I searched every aisle looking for where the two people had possibly gone, but it was useless. They were nowhere to be found.

I've been back to that very same Giant supermarket several times since, hoping that I might find answers or perhaps evidence to suggest a dimensional time warp of sorts, but it's all just wishful desire. I've never found anything quite as remarkable, aside from a moldy piece of produce or incorrect price labeling, which is becoming more frequent than UFO sightings these days.

A Fight with a Friend

I'd like to find more stories from those that have undergone similar time loop experiences, but uncovering first-hand testimony is just as rare as the time loop phenomenon itself. Sure, there are anecdotes here and there in a variety of books or publications, but I want to hear it from the people themselves, instead of just second- or third-hand accounts.

My wish was granted after I connected with Jan Harzan, the international director of the Mutual UFO Network (MUFON), the largest worldwide reporting and investigating organization of its kind that looks into the UFO phenomenon. It was an experience that stood out to him as very strange and unsettling. He further described it similarly to the 1993 film, *Groundhog Day,* in which the main character, played by Bill Murray, gets stuck in a time loop and undergoes the same course of events until he re-examines his own life and priorities.

Jan was between ten to twelve years of age when he walked out the front door of his home, catching sight of the next-door neighbor kid approaching as he neared his driveway. The two of them exchanged words, which soon developed into a disagreement for whatever reason, which quickly escalated into an all-out fistfight. Jan remembers throwing the boy into a ditch between their two houses and jumping on top of him.

But before the altercation ended, the next thing Jan recalls is again walking out his front door exactly as it had just taken place moments prior. And much to his surprise, the entire event replayed itself out in the exact same way he had already experienced. Having the information of what was about to take place again, Jan was fully aware of everything that was about to transpire, right down to the exact words spoken and movements made by each of them. He mentioned that in the moment, the thought did cross his mind at the time— "I wonder if I can change this." But another thought also crossed his mind shortly after— "Well if I do, then I will never know if it is going to be the same."[14]

The Parking Lot Premonition

How do we know for sure that the thoughts emanating from within us are actually originating within us? Perhaps it is possible to pick up on somebody else's precognitive experience, even if by mistake. After one unpleasant, first-hand experience I now think that is certainly possible.

There is one giant telecommunications provider that I'm definitely not a fan of. In fact, I refuse to ever use them again following a series of unfortunate customer service nightmares which occurred in the past. Many of my east coast readers can probably relate without diving into the details of this particular company's notorious service record—or rather, lack thereof.

Nevertheless, I was instructed to drive to one of their facilities to explain an issue to the half-wit behind the bulletproof glass as to why I was getting billed for a cable box I never owned to begin with. The other half-wit at the customer call center provided information to the contrary. This in turn led to an equally aggravating experience trying to sort out a matter of intelligence between two individuals that clearly had none whatsoever. My first tip-off should have been the bulletproof glass—an indicator of how upset customers have become in the past with this company.

At the moment where I found myself on the phone with one representative telling me one thing and face-to-face with another representative telling me another, I realized I was doomed to lose this battle and should just give up, before I beat my head upon the bulletproof glass in an attempt to wake myself up from the nightmare. But since I'm not a quitter and equally devoid of the common-sense logic I desired, I decided to stay, in the hopes all could eventually, somehow be sorted out.

I had a better chance at seeing a Sasquatch enter the facility before that ever happened.

14 Harzan, Jan. Email interview. 12 Dec. 2016.

Since I could only handle one idiot at a time, I hung up the phone just as another customer entered the facility to pick up their pre-packaged box of inevitable doom. The courteous person that I am, I gladly stepped off to the side to allow them the opportunity to jump into the fiery pits of digital disaster that awaited them.

Hanging out in the waiting room, I was enraged, but not surprised at the lack of service. It was now just a matter of waiting to be told for the umpteenth time by one dolt that I didn't owe anything and a couple weeks later receive another outrageous bill to the contrary.

I was still in my mood as another couple entered the waiting area behind that customer. But suddenly, I was hit with a different emotion—an overwhelming sense of dread. The notion immediately popped into my mind that my car was about to be hit in the parking lot of the damned place. It was not only an overwhelming sensation but also an undeniable one. I thought, but how could I get hit? It was a fairly large parking lot with plenty of room, plus the spot I had parked in was far enough from the road.

Just then, another individual entered the room and looked around frantically at us. He looked straight at me and asked, "Are you parked out here in the lot? I'm so sorry but I totally hit your car."

It was exactly what I did not need to have happen that day.

"You're the black Chevy, right?" the driver continued as I stood there stunned. He actually said some other make and model, which I don't recall exactly, but either way, it *wasn't my car.*

"Hey, that's my car!" said the first customer who had come in before the couple. He and the other driver ran outside to assess the damage.

Had I had a premonition intended for someone else? At the moment, I had been one hundred percent certain it was my car that was going to be hit, not somebody else's. Could my heightened emotional state have allowed the ideal conditions for such an experience to take place? I have often wondered what types of conditions can promote psychic abilities, and I have a suspicion that high emotion can certainly trigger it. But hijacking another person's premonition obviously intended for them? That's a new one.

Traci Bachmann, a schoolteacher in Philadelphia, related another experience that was eerily similar.[15] She had a dream where she was taking her three-year old son to pre-school, but was running late. As she brought

15 Bachmann, Traci. Personal interview. 11 Oct. 2016.

him into the building, she realized that she had left her pocketbook on the front seat of her car. Upon reaching her vehicle, she was pleasantly surprised to still find it there. However, upon closer inspection, she noticed that her purse had been completely torn apart and her wallet was stolen.

At that point, Traci woke up to her alarm clock to begin the real day. Ironically enough, she wasn't running late to her job, but cutting it close after dropping her son off to preschool earlier that morning. As she approached the entrance to the school she worked at, she noticed another teacher approaching from the other adjacent walkway.

The two teachers met at the door to buzz in and locked eyes in that moment. The other teacher exclaimed that she had left her phone directly on the front seat of her car and was concerned that it would get broken into again. Traci relayed the dream she had the night before and warned her colleague not to worry about being late to work, but to retrieve her possessions immediately.

It's worth noting that Traci had already been on edge from a school lockdown the day before the dream, where a man with a gun was supposedly spotted outside the school grounds. This was at the height of a widespread "creepy clown" phenomenon, where children and parents were reporting individuals dressed up in clown outfits spreading terror throughout the country.

"What a scenario, huh? Talk about being on the outermost fringes! Fringes so outermost that one didn't even know where the fringes were in relationship to anything else."[16]

– Ingo Swann

16 Swann, Ingo. "Grand Central Station." *Penetration: The Question of Extraterrestrial and Human Telepathy.* Kindle ed., Panta Rei/Crossroad Press, 2014. Location 1031-1039.

Stress and Supernatural Abilities

Perhaps stress plays a greater role in helping to promote these psychic experiences from the beginning.

A fair amount of people who exhibit psychic abilities say that they're best able to work when they are relaxed and not under a great deal of pressure. Psychic mediums I've worked with in the past describe their abilities as rendered useless or being "broken" when they can't pick up on anything due to a less-than-ideal working environment. A perfect example of this is when Uri Geller was featured on *The Tonight Show with Johnny Carson* in 1973.

Geller is probably one of the world's most well-known psychics, having been tested and validated several times by the Stanford Research Institute (SRI) as well as having worked with world governments in various espionage assignments. Geller was informed by the producers of *The Tonight Show* that he would be asked a series of questions before being asked to demonstrate his abilities, most notably the psychokinetic effects of which he is best known for. But at the very beginning of the interview, several objects were already waiting on a table in front of him along with an eager Johnny Carson who wasted no time in prompting him to perform his abilities.

Unfortunately, Geller didn't live up to the hype of the moment and the appearance is considered to be a flop. Those who have doubts of Geller's abilities are quick to use *The Tonight Show* failure as further proof of his fraudulence. But Geller has maintained that the Carson team purposely tried to trip him up and put him on the spot with a test he hadn't been prepared to do.[17]

In his *Tonight Show* appearance, Geller explained that many times nothing occurs unless he is in the right frame of mind or possesses a certain level of confidence. In the controlled experiments he did for SRI, Geller opted out of tests at times, particularly if he wasn't feeling confident in his ability. But when he was confident, the results were stunningly successful.

One double-blind experiment at SRI had Geller select from ten aluminum cans, one of which contained a particular object inside. The objects ranged from a ¾" steel ball bearing, a paper-wrapped bearing, a small magnet, a sugar cube, and room temperature water. Geller opted to pass on two of the tests because he didn't have adequate confidence in the moment, but in the other instances, he was correct twelve out of twelve times. According to SRI, this had a priori probability of a trillion to one. Another double-blind experiment contained a die that was placed inside a metal box. Again, Geller passed on two of the tests, but was correct eight out of eight times. SRI concluded this to be a probability of about one in a million.[18]

Given the pattern displayed by Geller in some of the SRI experiments, one could argue that Johnny Carson's insistence to get him to perform on live television created a stressful experience that rendered Geller unable to use his ability. Perhaps when the guest sitting next to Geller inadvertently touched the other objects on the table, or when Carson banged on his desk—these could have disrupted Geller's focus. But it wasn't a complete failure as Geller *was* able to bend one of the spoons, although just a little bit, which the cameras had captured. Unfortunately, it wasn't as impressive as Carson or the audience had hoped in the moment.[19]

It is easy to say that if Geller was a fraud, he was unable to perform his abilities because he didn't have time to prepare the illusion. But, what if his abilities were legit? And what if the stress of being on the national stage was too much for him to take? Should we discount every other successful example of his abilities simply because of this one instance where it wasn't?

---

17 *The Secret Life Of Uri Geller - Psychic Spy?* Directed by Vikram Jayanti, Spring Films/VIXPIX Films/British Broadcasting Corporation, 21 Jul. 2013.

18 "Summary of the SRI experiments." *UriGeller.com.* On Limited. 2017. Web. 23 Oct. 2017. http://www.urigeller.com/documentaries/summary-of-the-sri-experiments

19 *The Tonight Show Starring Johnny Carson.* NBC. Burbank, California. 01 Aug. 1973. Television.

On the other hand, stress sometimes enhances these abilities. Especially the more inadvertent abilities some people are not even aware they possess. I have often wondered if there is a connection to stress and inadvertent psychic ability. I've come to this notion after seeing some inexplicable events take place first-hand, as well as hearing numerous stories from individuals that are concurrently dealing with stressful situations in their life.

Take poltergeist cases, for example. The poltergeist phenomena typically involve recurrent spontaneous psychokinesis (RSPK). Events such as electrical interference, objects levitating or being thrown, disappearing and reappearing objects, apports*, or physical attacks and assaults by phantom presences are classic signs of a poltergeist. These events can last anywhere from a couple days, to a couple months, to a couple years in the extremely rare instance. But then in an instant, all activity completely and rather suddenly ceases.

*The sudden appearance of objects, which seemingly emerge out of thin air.

One theory among several paranormal researchers and parapsychologists is that these types of experiences could be linked to the wild, uncontrollable hormones in both boys and girls approaching puberty. Usually these poltergeist agents, as they are often referred to as (or those who are at the center of the phenomenon), do not have an outlet to channel their mental and emotional energy in a more productive way. Remove the poltergeist agent from the environment and the activity ceases. Bring them back in and it picks up again.

But it's not just pre-pubescent kids that are magnets for poltergeist activity. The same effects seem to plague adults who are also enduring great amounts of stress or trauma in their lives. We see this a lot with abused or troubled individuals too.

Loyd Auerbach, a professor of the paranormal with a master's degree in parapsychology from John F. Kennedy University, has taken the poltergeist phenomena to another level. He notes that unconscious movements seemed to be tied to the psychology of psychokinesis (PK) in a big way. Poltergeists are not spirits at all, but rather a living person's unconscious that causes it. It can happen either as a direct result of stress in an individual's life, which he calls a "telekinetic temper tantrum," or in a percentage of the cases where there seems to be a unique tie-in to their neurological state. In some of the instances, the poltergeist agents suffer from epilepsy or epileptic form activity.[20] Is it possible that the activity which manifests during a poltergeist, might be a response to or a by-product of an epileptic seizure?

Stress-Induced Psychokinetic Discharge

On more than one occasion, I had observed that Carrie expressed this similar form of heightened stress levels manifesting into a form of inadvertent psychic abilities.

It appeared that she was able to directly influence electronic instruments in a negative manner whenever she was extremely stressed, causing almost any device she touched to either glitch up or outright fail immediately or shortly thereafter. In fact, she had to replace numerous gadgets, especially laptops and cell phones, leaving her quite annoyed and often the butt of jokes relating to her electronic touch of death. Needless to say, many a night was spent holed up in a library somewhere, far from the theoretical death ray whenever I was on her bad side.

It resulted in being unfairly labeled a "black thumb" too because anything she planted or gardened quickly perished, usually within a short time frame if not immediately after planting. This led me to suspect that somehow Carrie's touch was giving off a psychokinetic discharge in moments of high stress. Her and others like her have also exhibited this ability, which I like to refer to as *stress-induced psychokinetic discharge* (SIPD).

Perhaps Carrie and others like her have a build-up of static electricity running through their bodies—although I have never witnessed a physically noticeable effect, such as walking a heavily carpeted surface then touching metal. At the time I lived with Carrie, I observed a direct correlation to the stress she endured in both professional and personal settings. A lot of the technical malfunctions seemed to correlate with either of these two things, or both, as the effects took place during a work-related or family dilemma. It soon developed into a rather comical take, especially if she were angry with me. She'd threaten to use my computer or phone in order to get even.

20 *Midnight in the Desert.* Dark Matter Digital Network / Roland Network Communications, 15 Sept. 2015.

If I had this ability, I'd probably have fun with it too. (At the very least, it's important to be able to still laugh about these things.)

In other examples where an electronic device failed in Carrie's hands, she would typically hand it off to me to figure out what was wrong with it. Oddly, the device would almost instantaneously begin to function normally again. Early on, this was confusing before we gave credence to the SIPD hypothesis. At one point, Carrie thought that she was tech illiterate and wondered if she broke things on account of her own ignorance. But that wasn't the case at all since she is in fact quite adept with technology, even referred to as the resident tech guru at one point in her career.

In a truly bizarre event, Carrie and I were at the gym one evening. She just got out of work and was overcome by a stressful situation earlier in the day. I suggested she share her frustrations in a more productive manner by running away from them on the treadmill, so I could listen to her vent while we both worked out.

As she started relaying the annoyances of the day, her treadmill abruptly shut down mid-stride. Thinking that it was merely a coincidence, I laughed it off to the SIPD again and suggested that we each shift down one machine, so she could take the treadmill I was on, which I knew operated correctly, and I'd take the other one next to it. We did just that, and then she continued her story. Only a few minutes passed when then that machine abruptly shut down too.

"Third time's a charm?" I quipped, and we slid down to the next set of machines. Soon enough as she began into her story again, that new machine also abruptly shut down. We decided we had gotten in all that we were going to get in with our brief workout and left.

Another individual, who I'll call "Emma" to preserve her requested anonymity, also has this innate ability to let stress levels influence not just small electronic gadgets, but much larger ones along with non-electronic objects in general.

Emma first started to become aware of her unwanted gifts after we began to converse and I quickly noticed the parallels between her life and Carrie's. It was also when Emma would be thinking about a stressful situation—particularly the toxic job environment she had been trying to escape or various failed relationships—that these abilities would seem to manifest.

One workday while sitting in her parked car, Emma was deciding between two different job offers she received, which stressed her out. As she reflected on the options, she simultaneously focused on a tiny spot on the windshield of her car. Suddenly the tiny spot rapidly developed into a large crack in the glass right before her eyes. Now one can argue that it might have been a drastic temperature fluctuation combined with a small chip that already existed in the windshield prior. This is in essence how a stress crack typically develops. Yet it is through the similarities between subsequent events that were to transpire later on in Emma's personal life that these seemingly innocuous trigger events could hardly be overlooked.

There were multiple times that her relatively new car would break down or stall out in the middle of an intersection after she fixated on stressful thoughts. Mechanics could never seem to pinpoint a mechanical issue either, which certainly didn't help out her already stressed state of mind. Usually after she talked with the repair shop by phone, these same people would no longer notify her about when the car would be ready for pickup. Yet it wasn't because they were rude, but as she would later discover, the phone lines at the repair shop would inexplicably stop functioning after her call!

Various appliances, electronics and even light bulbs would also fail after she had been stressed about her on-again, off-again boyfriend. During one break-up, Emma's cable box broke down the exact day they split. The cable company informed her that they could not locate the source of the malfunction to accurately troubleshoot it, so they replaced the entire unit instead. At another point, Emma had her debit card stolen—an already extremely difficult situation in itself. She went to the bank the following day to have them close the connected account and reissue a new one. However, the bank's computer system abruptly crashed in the midst of issuing her the new card. Later on, while they attempted to print the new card, their printer spewed uncharacteristic yellow splotches instead. In an amused manner, layered within a hint of genuine concern, Emma informed the bank teller that it was probably her "supernatural powers" interfering with their system. The bank teller laughed it off at first, but by the fourth attempt to print the new card, the teller reconsidered the theory by exclaiming, "I don't understand. This has never happened before."[21] But to Emma, it was no different than the other SIPD instances she had experienced and still experiences to this day.

21 "Emma." Correspondences conducted via text messaging, phone calls and in-person interviews. 2014-2015.

Occasionally I'll hear about college students who experience activity in their dorms. Not the obvious dorm room antics that go bump in the night, but rather that of the unexplained variety. There is of course the standard fare of spooky legends, which creep up across campuses all the time. Yet in a small handful of college cases, they seem to be isolated to the students themselves, which could hint at another possible stress-induced scenario instead.

One email I received was from a student living on campus at Shippensburg University of Pennsylvania. This young woman genuinely believed her dorm room was haunted for a variety of reasons. Lights would turn on and off by themselves. Alarms would mysteriously go off in the middle of the night. Her roommate would frequently hear sounds of thumping from within their closet along with phantom whispers. She explained that the microwave would sound like it was spinning the round plate on its own without being on, or at certain times, exhibit a growling that could be heard from within the microwave. Random items were knocked off of shelves or would be in different places from the night before.

Potential demonic or mischievous infestation theories aside, what else could possibly be causing her and her roommate to experience such activity?

I asked about her experiences prior to enrollment at the school and learned that both she and her roommate hadn't been a stranger to paranormal activity. Both of them experienced strange occurrences all throughout their lives. After I suggested some of the usual empowering tips in an attempt to minimize the activity (which I'm assuming was successful, as I never heard back from them again) I began to think more about the SIPD connection.

The students could be inadvertently triggering disturbances based on their heightened stress levels too. Supernatural events might take place more often when they cram for a test, are worried about project deadlines, deal with finances, relationships, or one of the several other issues students endure in their college careers. I hope that someone might survey a large student population and look for correlations between paranormal activity and stress.

I'd also speculate that perhaps the collective consciousness between groups of students (and maybe even those with more instances of paranormal experiences *before* they get to college) could somehow act as a trigger that goes off in unison with other experiencers.

Shared Connections

We now know that stress affects our physiological makeup and impacts our ability to deal with illness and disease, so it should come as no surprise when it affects other aspects of our physical and metaphysical environments too. It appears that we can also connect with people on a psychical level, especially if we are close with them.

I was at the shopping mall in King of Prussia, Pennsylvania (one of the largest shopping malls in the country) with a woman I had begun seeing named Rachael who has a distinct foreign accent. As she went into a greeting card store, I mentioned that I'd meet her back inside the shop after I made my way to the adjacent food court for a quick beverage. But when I came back, I did not see her inside the shop. My initial thought of having to track her down in such an enormous shopping mall was not appealing whatsoever.

It was in that very moment I suddenly heard Rachael shout—*HEY*—in her distinct tone.

The voice was loud enough to startle me, which doesn't happen often. I spun around immediately, although I could not discern in what direction the shout had actually emanated from. I remember the voice being so loud and audible that it sounded like it had enveloped me from many directions. I had never experienced anything quite like that before.

A few seconds later, I saw Rachael walk out of the greeting card store, quite calm in comparison to my confused state. She immediately picked up on my visual cues and asked what was wrong. I explained that I heard her voice right before she exited the shop, but she insisted that it wasn't her. At first, I didn't buy it because it was distinctly her tone, but she swore that it hadn't been her. Had we shared a non-verbal psychical exchange in that quick moment when I was stressed? And why hadn't I initially seen her in the store that I later saw her walk out of?

This correlation between heightened emotional states could be a driving force in paranormal experiences taking place. However, it may not be triggered by just negative or stressful energy, but positive energy too.

The conversations with my neighbor Nick generally cover a wide variety of topics—from the metaphysical, to theological, to hip-hop. For whatever reason we've shared numerous collective telepathic experiences too. For example, in the midst of our dialog, an obscure memory popped into my head. Without mentioning how it came to me, I just shared the memory. Nick stopped me and said, "I was literally thinking of that same exact thing, moments before you even started talking about it!"

Another time I was eating at the dinner table when I felt an urge to get the camera on my phone ready. I had a strong feeling that Nick would come to my back door to show me the anomalous lights in the sky he had been seeing on a number of occasions. Sure enough, within the same minute of getting that impression, I received the knock on my door and the invitation to photograph the lights in the sky that he saw.

Nick has an impressive ability to freestyle rap, so I occasionally ghostwrite lyrics for him. Songwriting is a great stress reliever for me, so I take enjoyment in being able to expand my creativity to another realm and help someone else out in his or her own creative endeavors. One night while doing this, an overwhelming set of lyrics came over me that became an entire song within the hour. This was highly unusual for me. I messaged Nick to come over if he was free, so I could share it with him, unaware that the lyrics I penned struck a personal chord with him. The lyrics revealed personal details about him that I hadn't known previously. And yet somehow in the moment when I wrote them, I felt like I was in the mindset of someone else. I suppose I had picked up on Nick's thoughts the entire time, as the lyrics directly referenced a social situation he was in at the very same moment they came to me.

But the strangest event between the two of us took place on another occasion, when I had been expecting him in the first place. I heard a clear set of knocks on the back door, but when I opened it, there was no one there. When I shut the door again, I heard the same set of knocks on the front door. When I answered the front door, there was Nick waiting there ready to come in.

I asked him if he had knocked on the back door just a few moments prior. "No," he replied, "but I actually thought about it moments *before* coming to the front door."

The Lingering Chirping

The age-old statement we hear from science: energy can neither be created nor destroyed. For whatever reason the same concept appears to be relevant in the paranormal spectrum as well. This is also the case when immediate or unexpected "ends" of energy result and leave behind an imprint in our perceived reality.

It is this same principle that could apply to why hauntings tend to be centered on sudden or tragic deaths, or even in areas that were prone to intense emotion. All the energy contained in one spot—the event, the people associated with it, even the ambient sounds relevant to the moment—could be collected and stored, then played back like a recording on an infinite loop. It's what paranormal investigators refer to as the *stone tape theory.*

This brings up another point to ponder on the essence of time itself and whether or not there is actually a beginning or an end or if it always is. The elimination of time as a linear concept is one that is now being considered by theoretical physicists as they look at the possibilities of a multiverse. Or in other words, a universe that contains many realities, co-existing within one another, albeit sometimes overlapping.

In college, Carrie lived in a converted building with some roommates in downtown Lancaster, Pennsylvania, along with two cats and a parakeet named Petey. I had become quite fond of Petey, especially in the delightful chirping that came from the living room where his cage was.

As I came home with Carrie one day, we noticed the birdcage was knocked on the floor and one of the cats was locked inside of it. Petey was nowhere to be found apart from a flurry of feathers scattered everywhere. At that point, we were not so much concerned with figuring out how such a cat found herself trapped inside a birdcage, but rather if the cage's previous tenant was still alive. Sadly, it was not, as Carrie quickly discovered Petey's decapitated body in another part of the house.

I chose to sit by myself in the living room in disbelief that such a turn for the worst could take place with what otherwise seemed like two well-behaved cats. My mind was in a stressful state, as I stared onto the now empty birdcage in the corner of the living room. It was in that moment that I began to hear a faint chirp from the corner where the cage had been. The sound never became any louder or more frequent. It was just a steady, consistent chirp. But it was distinctly Petey's, which I had become accustomed to before. I was in awe for several minutes. Was I hallucinating? I called in Carrie to confirm the sound and she too heard it.

Had it been the ghost of Petey or a lingering impression of residual energy? Perhaps another Petey still existed, but in a reality where he was no longer physically present within our own.

"Humanity is more or less like we're in a little tidal pool on the edge of the ocean. We've reached a lot of really strong conclusions about what the ocean is like and what sort of creatures live there... without ever actually having been there."[22]

– Richard Beckwith

22 "Richard Beckwith, Wyoming's UFO Hunting Lawyer." *Open Minds UFO Radio.* Open Minds Production/Blog Talk Radio, 03 Oct. 2017.

Oh, the Many Varied Viewpoints

Different people approach the topic of ghosts in different ways. From the scientific approach, to the spiritual implications, to the technological aspects, there can be a multitude of varied opinions on what is seemingly correct and not correct about it. For some, the whole subject is just plain terrifying and for others, it's merely laughable at best. Since the study of anomalous phenomena isn't an exact science, nor is there a definitive answer to explain away all the mysteries of the cosmos, there surely cannot be just one right or wrong way to study it.

So then how can we grow in our understanding of this very complex topic?

Perhaps we can start by not necessarily being so focused on figuring it all out, but rather just observing it for what it is. Much of this curious phenomenon seems to have no desire in ever being completely figured out anyway. When we begin to take note of patterns and commonalities in how it operates, some theories start to hold more weight than others and connections can then be drawn towards any sort of possible conclusion.

However, it would seem that those involved with the study of high strangeness are often reluctant to commit themselves to a specific religion at times too. Maybe they don't want to disrupt the balance in their personal relationships with people, or maybe they think such a specific faith alignment could hinder their studies, or perhaps it could convey the wrong connotations of an evangelical crusade.

My objective is not to convince someone one way or another in what perspective they should take. Spiritual journeys are unique to the individual feet that walk them. If I can get a person to start asking questions, then maybe I've helped them to lace up their shoes, at the very least. Even though I approach the phenomena from a Christian perspective, it doesn't imply that I have it all figured out either.

My paralleling interest in both theology and the supernatural can either leave an encouraging effect or a troubling one, especially towards other Christians I've met along the way. Some are curious in how my pursuit of one might influence my perspective in the other, albeit in a negative way. To be honest, it has actually strengthened it.

Reincarnation, Parallel Realities and the Multiverse Mouthful

The concept of reincarnation can be a touchy subject, depending on where someone is at in his or her own faith. This notion may or may not play nicely with it. There are convincing arguments for and convincing arguments against the subject. Usually the most convincing body of evidence draws from individuals with vivid recollections of past lives. But what about the instances where people also report future lives as well? How does that fit into the view of "recycled souls?"

Demonic influence is one possibility to explain why people think they've had previous lives. Disembodied entities could be feeding information in an attempt to confuse and deceive. Psychologist, Dr. Edith Fiore looked into this aspect with her book titled, *The Unquiet Dead*, which seemed to suggest spirit possession as the more plausible explanation.

But well-known paranormal investigator Paul F. Eno once said, "When you don't have a past and a future in an objective sense, you can't have past lives."[23] So could all of this reincarnation talk better fit into the multiverse model instead?

The multiverse theorizes that there are multiple versions of us living out there in a different reality, but concurrent with our own reality. And every conscious choice that we make creates an alternative scenario based on other choices we didn't make, which continue on existing and making their independent choices, which give birth to other realities and existences based on those choices, and so on and so forth into an infinite realm of

---

23 *Coast to Coast AM*. Premiere Radio Networks, 09 Jun. 2007.

endless possibilities and outcomes. No wonder it's so hard to time travel. To what time and reality do we travel?

Paranormal theory suggests that every so often these alternate realities could overlap into our seemingly present and current reality and then strangeness ensues. One aspect of the strangeness could be identified as the ghost phenomenon, because for the people that are experiencing it, this might be how the overlap appears to them. Eno discusses two instances that stand out as prime examples of this concept. One of which he refers to as "the almost suicide case" from Oxford, Massachusetts.[24]

When Eno went to check on a farmhouse that had paranormal activity, he noticed a strong psychical sense of suicide, in and around the upstairs bathroom, yet nowhere else on the property. Eno also sensed the influence of what he calls paranormal *parasites* throughout the house, but nowhere else did he pick up on the strong impression as he did whenever he was near the bathroom. Eno asked the woman who lived there—a single mother with several children—if anyone had committed suicide in the bathroom. The woman looked at him oddly. Not because it was an outlandish question, but because she had seriously considered suicide in that specific location. She considered it a place where an adult cousin would find her instead of her own children. In multiverse theory, all possibilities exist. So, in that alternate reality, maybe the woman did commit suicide in the bathroom.

Maybe this energy that is given off into the multiverse is also used as a source of "food" for these parasitic negative entities to feed from. And as they feed, they grow in strength in order to manifest. In that case, Eno thought that the invisible parasite wasn't getting enough to feed off of and was just tied to the negative energy in the bathroom. Maybe it reached out to the other occupants in the house in order to feed on more negative energy and gain more strength, which could explain why activity was occurring all throughout the property instead of just in the bathroom.

As investigators looking into these types of cases, we should try and discover where the initial source of negative energy was first conceptualized as a means to discover where and when the activity originated. That might point us in a more accurate direction to better assess and diagnosis the level to which the negative parasite has grown and hopefully put a stop to it.

---

24 *Coast to Coast AM*. Premiere Radio Networks, 09 Jun. 2007.

Another example in the multiverse ghost connection is a case that Eno references from 1978.[25] He received a phone call from a University of Connecticut student, who relayed the story of how she, her youngest sister, and some friends had been driving through the village of York, Maine, at the time. As they passed a ranch house off in the distance, the young woman's sister became excited and exclaimed that the house was actually her house. After she insisted they stop the car, she jumped out of the vehicle and ran up to the front door.

A woman in her forties screamed when she opened the door to find the unannounced visitor standing there. Her husband quickly came out and was surprised too. The girl answered, "Look, I'm sorry to intrude but I really felt as though I knew this house." The man replied, "You *should* know this house. You haunt it."[26]

Later, when Eno researched the name and address on the mailbox that the young woman happened to write down as they left the property. He wrote the homeowners a letter with his contact information, should they ever want to get in touch with him about the incident. The husband called Eno three days later to reveal how he and his wife had seen a girl in transparent form frequently moving about their house, particularly coming down the steps and looking out the front window, among other things.

Separately, Eno interviewed the young woman who had claimed she knew the house. She explained that she had dreams of being in the house and doing precisely what the couple explained the ghost had been doing. But her and the couple had never conversed or met after that one unannounced visit. They only talked to Eno about the incidents and not to each other.

When the girl arrived at the house that day, she said the first thought that popped into her mind as she took note of the property was, "Why aren't there any toys in the yard?"[27] In her dreams, she was the mother of two children living there and it appeared to be her house. She would look out the front window to keep an eye on her children, which is exactly what the couple relayed. In their interview with Eno, the couple had explained

25 *Midnight in the Desert*. Dark Matter Digital Network / Roland Network Communications, 18 Apr. 2016.

26 *Midnight in the Desert*. Dark Matter Digital Network / Roland Network Communications, 18 Apr. 2016.

27 *Midnight in the Desert*. Dark Matter Digital Network / Roland Network Communications, 18 Apr. 2016.

that it was almost like the ghost was looking through them, not at them. And yet what's even more curious about the entire ordeal is that after the girl and the couple met on that porch that strange day, all ghostly phenomena and dreams ceased immediately thereafter.

Radio host Dave Schrader recalls another similar story that was told to him by a listener of his show.[28] The listener relayed how his grandparents had bought a plot of land to build a house on, which didn't have any of the usual catalysts associated with it that paranormal investigators have come to believe trigger hauntings. Nobody ever died in the house. Nor were there any deaths or strange events associated with the property. The house wasn't built upon an Indian burial ground. And everything that was bought for the house was also brand new so there wasn't even a shred of strange energy attached to any of the objects in there.[29]

But the man recalled a time when the grandmother thought otherwise. She relayed that while she was in her recliner in the living room watching TV during daylight hours, three shadow figures walked into the room, stopped in front of her, then quickly turned and ran out of the room. A few years later, the grandmother passed away and the man took over the house. Two of his friends came over to visit. As the three of them entered the living room, they saw the full-bodied apparition of his grandmother sitting there in the recliner. The three friends stared at her, then quickly turned and ran out of the room.

Now who is really haunting who?

By-Products of Heightened Awareness

Let's say you purchase a brand new, red sports car. Soon, everywhere you look, you notice red sports cars in the same make and model and think, "Who knew there were this many of them on the road?" They were always there to begin with; it's just that you didn't notice since they didn't concern you at the time. Now that you had tuned yourself into recognizing

28 *Midnight in the Desert.* Dark Matter Digital Network / Roland Network Communications, 23 May 2018.

29 *Midnight in the Desert.* Dark Matter Digital Network / Roland Network Communications, 15 Jun. 2018.

all the red sports cars, the sight appears more common, simply because you became more aware to the reality of it.

Whenever someone focuses on the paranormal, it can lead to an ultra-awareness of the spectrum, which results in some truly exciting occurrences—or frightening, depending on the intensity. An individual could easily mistake these occurrences as the result of either inviting something into their environment or suddenly becoming a magnet for it, when it could be that the activity was always there to begin with; it's just that the individual has become more aware of its existence.

One disturbing story as a result of this heightened awareness was told to me by a Buddhist follower named Hyejin. She began to see the spirits of the deceased on her path towards enlightenment. The individual that introduced us knew of my longtime interest in the subject of ghosts and was eager to get Hyejin to talk about her own experiences, which at first, she had been very reluctant to speak about. This is often the case with those who have genuine experiences but are also very afraid of them. It takes some time and patience for them to feel comfortable enough to open up and talk about it.

Hyejin told me that this by-product of seeing the dead was part of the process of her spiritual journey, as her Buddhist teachers explained. The teachers said the ability would subside over time but stressed that she should not focus on that particular aspect, lest it take longer to eventually subside.[30]

When explaining these encounters, Hyejin would point to the middle of her forehead, just above the eyebrows, where she would feel intense pain, especially in the moments leading up to an experience. It was in that moment that she would also feel weak, almost as if such an entity was drawing upon her and sucking out her energy in order to manifest. Sometimes the entities would eventually also become aware of her and physically approach her. This part freaked her out a great deal, so she would cover her eyes and just wish them away. Driving on the highway was an exceptionally harrowing experience, especially when driving by a car wreck. She would see the spirits of the presumably deceased walking about the scene and not looking so pretty either.[31]

After our initial conversation, I never saw Hyejin again. We corresponded only briefly one other time after that, but her experiences

30 Hyejin. Personal interview. 08 Aug. 2010.

31 Hyejin. Personal interview. 08 Aug. 2010.

were never spoken about or brought up. I only hope that somehow, she was able to turn off this ability instead of having it plague her forever.

This reminds me of another individual I corresponded with in the past. Katie was a college student who had just started to discover that she could speak with this unseen realm. From what Katie explained later on, there would be moments when she was in class and suddenly she would hear a buzzing in her ear. She described it as kind of like feedback from a microphone close to a speaker. To her, this implied that someone from the other side wanted to speak with her and get a message across. This quickly became distracting and intense enough that Katie would have to leave the classroom for several moments at a time. This constant interaction would make Katie very tired and she would even spend an entire day recovering from it on both a mental and physical level.[32]

The Medical Community

One supernatural occurrence that generates a lot of interest is the near-death experience (NDE). It is something that a number of people within the medical community can certainly attest to and yet at the same time have difficulty accepting. And it is often this same community of trained professionals that have a tough time going on the public record to talk about other things they cannot explain. There are a number of these unexplained events that take place in hospitals, especially from what I've been told. But the true unexplained aspect is why more don't come out and talk about it.

Fear of reprisal or backlash from their peers is a very powerful deterrent. Few have actually come out and gone on the record to talk about it and those that do are usually ridiculed or jeopardize their careers. One such encounter involves a young woman by the name of "Ria Baker," a medical student in the midst of her residency who is also an *empath*. This is someone who has an awareness to sense (and often become overwhelmed with) strong emotion picked up from other people or energy in the vicinity within a particular environment.

Ria worked the overnight shift at a hospital in the Lehigh Valley area of Pennsylvania. A man in his thirties had overdosed on heroin and was

32 Katie. Correspondences conducted via electronic messaging. Oct. 2010.

brought in unconscious. It was suspected the man had undergone violent seizures since first responders discovered his body contorted in an awkward position. Ria was on shift at that time and saw him come into the ER and into surgery.

Later that same night, between the hours of 1:00 am and 2:00 am, Ria walked the floors checking in on the patients, when she noticed the same man out in the hall by the window. This time the man was in a wheelchair and just staring down into his lap. She approached him and asked, "Can I do anything for you?" The man looked up at her with sad eyes and just shook his head.*

*Ria had told me about this experience twice—once in person a couple days after the event had taken place and again several months later so that I could record it for this book. When Ria had initially told me about this encounter, she mentioned that the man said, "You can't help me" or something to that extent. Today, she doesn't recall if he said something or not, but believes the strong possibility he might have. Beyond that the rest of her account remains consistent with the first time I heard it.

For some reason, she simply patted the man on the shoulder and walked away. Although she admits, this is not something she would usually do in this instance. Usually she would have taken him back to his room or gotten another nurse to assist. Twenty minutes later, Ria heard "code blue" over the intercom system, which is a cardiac arrest alert. The room number that she was called to happened to be the same room number as the man that was brought in for surgery—the same man that she had seen moments prior in the wheelchair.

As the sun came up and her shift came to an end, Ria went on her usual rounds with the morning team and noticed the man in his room. According to the records, he was resuscitated and was placed on a ventilator during the surgery, but never came off it. "He looked like hell—his eyes were open and moving but he was nonresponsive," according to her account.[33] The man also had had both his legs amputated to the knee and one arm amputated to the elbow. But the records indicated he had been nonresponsive since after the surgery ended—which would have been around 11:00 pm.

Ria stressed that there was no way this very same man, who was seen by her in a wheelchair hours later in the night, could have been out in the hall responding to her. Especially not with all of his limbs still intact either. The man hadn't been responsive in any way, other than basic reflexes, and

33 "Baker, Ria." Interview conducted via electronic messaging. 19 Jan. 2017.

most likely suffered anoxic brain damage (oxygen deprivation) somewhere between taking the heroin and then being picked up by first responders.

It seems that what Ria had encountered was a ghost of some sort, but not in the classic sense that ghosts are often thought of. In this case, it was not the spirit of a deceased individual, but rather a conscious or subconscious manifestation of an individual projected into one space, while the physical body was in another. This would be, in an equal sense, a perfect example of bilocality, which is often reported during incidents of *crisis apparitions.*

A crisis apparition is typically reported when an individual goes through something quite traumatic and someone else related to them or who knows them very well, physically sees that individual somewhere else. The crisis apparition can be observed several miles from the spot where the crisis had been occurring at the exact same moment it had been taking place.

But Ria had never met this man before in her life. So why was she the seemingly only one who had witnessed the manifestation and even interacted with it? Stranger still is the fact that Ria is surprised she didn't think it was bizarre to begin with when she initially saw the man out in the hall. Because, as she puts it, "there was absolutely no way he could have been that healthy after what he'd been through."[34]

But more puzzling was why Ria seemingly acted out of character in that moment by simply patting the man on the shoulder, then leaving. Unless of course, the phenomenon has the capability to subtly and covertly influence us in ways that we aren't even aware of.

Subtle Manipulation

I have begun to draw a connection in paranormal occurrences: the people experiencing them also seem to act out of character in comparison to how they would normally respond to such circumstances.

It is a curious observation that leads me to believe there is something just as important and worth noting in the ordinary, so much as we take note of what lies in the extraordinary. On investigations, we should start asking people *why* they responded in the way that they did in the moments

34 "Baker, Ria." Interview conducted via electronic messaging. 19 Jan. 2017.

immediately following the supernatural occurrence. You might be just as surprised as the individuals themselves when they begin to realize that perhaps it was an odd way to *not* react as opposed to how they know they would have reacted in any other circumstance.

Then again, it should come as no surprise to the trained researcher as these forces are: not always as they appear to be; masterfully deceptive, and equally as manipulative.

It is even common in UFO reports to hear the witness state that they suddenly had an overwhelming desire to look up towards the sky, where a craft or anomalous object is already there waiting for them. This begs the question, do we have a deeper connection to this phenomenon that we are unaware of, or does it seem to have some sort of control over us?

To the contrary, there also appears to be an inclination to not pay any attention to the phenomenon too.

In March of 1997, residents from the city of Phoenix, Arizona reported a number of lights in the sky, along with delta-shaped and triangular craft spotted in and around the region. Most UFO buffs recall the mass sighting that took place on March 13th, which mainstream media covered—three months after the fact—but a lot of the activity occurred in the weeks prior. Some of the witnesses relayed how, instead of being in sheer awe of their encounters or immediately wanting to share their experience with others, they instead found themselves in a sort of temporary amnesia.

Investigative filmmaker James Fox told of how some hospice workers who were present at the time to actually see the lights appear and disappear, didn't mention a single word about it during the actual event. Fox said that one woman told him, "We went right back to our tea."[35] Acting director of Arizona MUFON, Jim Mann, claims that he spoke to an individual that reported stopping the car on the side of the road and watching with several others who did the same thing as a craft "slowly glided overhead.

35 Open Minds Production. "James Fox – The Phoenix Lights 20 Years Later: Meet the Witnesses and Hear New Information." *International UFO Congress Lectures and Videos, Open Minds Production/2017 International UFO Congress,* 27 Feb. 2017. https://openminds.pivotshare.com/media/james-fox-the-phoenix-lights-20-years-later%3A-meet-the-witnesses-and-hear-new-information/59734/feature

Not a word was spoken. After it went on by, everyone got in their car and drove home."[36]

Even actor Kurt Russell witnessed the lights in a uniform V-shape while he flew his private plane over the Phoenix airport that night. He radioed to the tower, who informed him that their radar systems were not showing any aircraft, but they logged the lights as unidentified. Russell thought nothing more of this until he saw a documentary on the Phoenix Lights, which stirred up memories of his own sighting. But when he went back to check his log books on the day of the flight, he had somehow forgotten to record the event.[37]

Governor Fife Symington came under great fire in how he initially dealt with the Phoenix Lights incident. Later that same year, he held an official press conference to reveal that the mystery had finally been solved. But this cheap stunt revealed nothing more than the governor's chief of staff dressed up in a ridiculous alien costume and identified as the lone culprit instead.

However, ten years later, Symington reversed his stance and went on the public record to say that on that same night of the mass sighting, he himself had witnessed a massive, delta-shaped craft navigate silently over Squaw Peak (a mountain range in Phoenix) and remarked that it was truly breathtaking.[38]

I'd like to give him the benefit of the doubt as he mentioned to CNN in 2007 that he didn't want to stir the pot and cause a panic—but is going to humorous lengths to dispel the mystery really the most effective way in achieving that? Especially if he too saw the same thing everyone else had seen? I wonder if Symington's reaction at the time was really an attempt to discredit the whole event—or if it was subtle manipulation by the forces behind the phenomenon, unbeknownst to him.

---

36 Haller, Sonja. "5 surprising things about the 'Phoenix Lights' sighting we learned at UFO Congress." *The Arizona Republic/azcentral.com,* 17 Feb. 2017. Web. 08 May 2017. http://www.azcentral.com/story/entertainment/events/2017/02/17/phoenix-lights-ufo-sighting-ugo-congress-scottsdale/98062066

37 Tingley, Brett. "Kurt Russell Recalls UFO Sighting in BBC Interview." *Mysterious Universe.* 8th Kind Pty Ltd. 28 Apr. 2017. Web. 02 Jul. 2018. http://mysteriousuniverse.org/2017/04/kurt-russell-recalls-ufo-sighting-in-bbc-interview

38 Symington, Fife. "Symington: I saw a UFO in the Arizona sky." *CNN,* Cable News Network/Turner Broadcasting System, 09 Nov. 2007. Web. 19 Jul. 2017. http://www.cnn.com/2007/TECH/science/11/09/simington.ufocommentary/index.html

Unwitting participants in the alien abduction experience can encounter mental manipulation plus a more painful, physical manipulation too. David Jacobs writes about how some of the entities involved in the abduction and monitoring process will routinely instill headaches into those who describe their experiences to researchers.[39] Since the abduction program is a rather covert one, where the abductors are in clear control, it doesn't surprise me that they would refrain from discussing their motives with us. Is it wishful thinking to hope they are here to help humanity, or are we being cleverly manipulated to believe that?

Another example of the subtle control over our cognitive behavior and reactionary responses can be found in EVP (electronic voice phenomena).* An illustration of this involves paranormal investigator Dan Webster, who captured an unknown female voice during an investigation that whispered, "Do you have to use the bathroom?" Even though he never heard the voice audibly at the time, he proclaimed to his investigative team seconds after the voice, saying, "I'm going to use the facilities first."[40]

*EVP is a popular technique among paranormal investigators for documenting ethereal entities. They are generally not heard during the recording process but are usually discovered upon playback and widely believed to be the "voices of the dead."

Now this brings up a few possibilities beyond the enigma of the EVP itself. Did this voice somehow know Dan was going to use the bathroom before he even considered it, or did the voice subtly suggest it to him? Perhaps the voice was tied to this physiological urge and therefore a projection of his consciousness instead. But if that was the case, then why was it a *female* voice?

Again, this example and so many others like it requires us to reevaluate what a ghost might actually be. No longer will the simple answer that it's the lingering energy of deceased individuals satisfy the question. But more importantly, what ability do these forces within the spectrum have to influence our thoughts and actions? It would seem that they could carry much more control over us than we often realize, and that's an even scarier proposition.

---

39 Jacobs, David M., PhD. "Integrated Hubrids—Violence." *Walking Among Us: The Alien Plan to Control Humanity.* Kindle ed., Disinformation Books-Red Wheel/Weiser, 2015. pg. 129.

40 Webster, Dan. Personal correspondences. 2016-2017.

The Haunted Therapist

Science wrestles with the validity of paranormal phenomena based on the grounds that it can be tested within the constrained parameters of our known physical universe. There are plenty of case reports that show this may in fact operate from outside of our known laws.

Let's go back to the health community, and more specifically, the mental health community. I would hope that in time more people within that field would consider the paranormal experience not just from a black and white viewpoint, but also a rather gray one. The philosophy that either an individual is experiencing something real, or they are just simply hallucinating, might not be the way to approach such a little understood phenomenon in general. After all, we don't know how exactly it operates. It could be altering the physical environment as well as the mental one.

Certain individuals might be experiencing legitimate paranormal phenomena, or they could be struggling with a severe mental condition. Then again, could they also be struggling with both? How can we tell where one ends and the other begins in a fringe subject where there is no distinct separation between its reality and ours? What if it's the medical evaluator that is struggling with the veil between the two worlds as well?

After Carrie and I had separated in a precursor to the eventual divorce, I began to meet with John; a mental health professional and an Episcopalian priest. John was one the kindest, most empathetic individuals I had ever met—a trait I'm sure he drew from the church—but to my surprise this clergyman also happened to be quite interested in the paranormal. His interest was fueled in part because he also had an ability to perceive the other side.

One morning in his office, I recounted the events that led up to the sudden death of Carrie's grandmother, and the funeral preparations that were arranged for the following day. When John and I shifted gears to the topics of spirituality and theology, he abruptly became quiet at one point. He glanced upwards and behind me in the direction of the far corner of the meeting room and I felt a cold breeze on my shoulder. "You'll have to forgive me, because there is a shape starting to take form in the corner of the room." John said.

My mind entertained the possibility that it was the spirit of Carrie's grandmother somehow drawn into our discussion. But John corrected me as if he was also picking up on my thoughts. "No, this is a man," he added.

John put his hand up to the side of his face, not wanting to see the form anymore. "It's not your time," he said to the unseen presence. He looked back at me, "It's your time to speak, Justin. I want to be fair to you. I don't know what this other guy wants, but it's not his time to speak."

I continued on. This had not been a new aspect in my conversations with John. When my interest in the paranormal was first brought up in our conversations, John felt like he could confide in me his ability to see these deceased entities. Though it didn't happen often, his ability allowed him to also deliver messages to his patients, cluing them in on certain aspects of their life that they were surprised to hear John bring up.

I considered that perhaps John had more of a telepathic ability, but he claimed that the visitors would tell him these things. So, he just delivered the message, whatever that message would entail. This allowed him to become extremely insightful with his patients, allowing them to discuss aspects to their problems they would have otherwise not brought up on their own.

In this case, John embraced an ability that most decide to reject, but he did not call it a gift. He considered himself just a conduit to the other side that was more than willing to do whatever God had given him the ability to do. Sometimes this meant confronting the spirits when the time wasn't right for them to be there.

The situation I found myself in at the time did not frighten nor surprise me. I knew I was safe in John's presence and figured the best thing would be to just talk normally as if nothing strange was happening at all. This is often the advice I pass on to others not wanting to attract the attention of these entities. Yet I could tell in the moment that John was still distracted with the uninvited guest. Eventually, he relaxed knowing that the man had finally left.

"Do you think it came for me?" I asked.

"No, because those who come for my patients, tend to stick around for a while, insistent that they stay. This man did not exhibit that," John explained.

"Did you have a patient earlier who may have lost someone recently?"

"No, but this man could have been brought in by somebody else. I don't know."

I was intrigued so I explored the notion further: "We were talking about some pretty heavy subject matter a few moments prior to the entity manifesting. Do you find that opening the dialogue to talking about this stuff brings these entities out?"

"Oh yes."

The Nature of Things

It's inevitable that as the world becomes attached to their possessions they will inevitably come to worship them too. Acquiring the latest and greatest has become the religion in a materialistic society. So, it should come as no surprise then that the tremendous mental energy invested into these objects has by some accounts empowered the very objects themselves to come alive in a sense. Then there are the reports of objects that can contain certain energies within them, or certain entities that have somehow become attached.

The well-known paranormal investigators, Ed and Lorraine Warren, collected and housed various artifacts from their investigations, which still remain stored in their "haunted museum" in Monroe, Connecticut. Decades later, the Syfy network chronicled their nephew John Zaffis doing the same in *The Haunted Collector*, a show which aired from 2011 through 2013.

Think about how many heirlooms have been passed down through generations of families. Think about how many people have difficulty giving up the clunker car that fails often or is quite unsafe because it's been with them throughout most of their lives. Think about how hard it is to say goodbye to something we've become accustomed to for so long since it feels like it's part of our very being. It is this obsession with inanimate physical objects that can be both fascinating and dangerous.

There is the theory that mirrors might be linked to an increase of paranormal activity. The tremendous amount of time we spend just gazing into them—admiring the beauty of its reflection or the repulsion of its flaws. We partake in this intense ritual day in and day out for most of our lives. Therefore, the theory is plausible that an inadvertent bit of projected psychic energy might somehow get trapped within a mirror, given the right conditions.

Could that same psychic energy somehow project back out into our own reality? On that same reflection, some paranormal investigators associate older mirrors to be more connected with haunting activity. Perhaps this can be attributed to the buildup of decades or centuries of intense mental energy released onto them. Or maybe it's just the physical make-up of the mirror itself. Back in the day, mirrors were covered with a thin sheet of mercury, tin or even silver. Could the combination of physical and metaphysical properties be an ideal conductor for such activity to be reflected back? This whole concept is purely speculative and something I've not had the time to test myself, but it leads me into a somewhat related example.

In 2005, my mother, Margie and her husband Rick, had an inexplicable encounter. It took place in a remodeled portion of their home that has now become their sunroom. The remodeling changed the way the door to the adjacent bathroom was opened and closed, which was opposite to the original construction of the house. It is not uncommon for people to experience paranormal activity during or directly after the remodeling process, and what transpired was just another example of this. They awoke one morning to what they thought initially had been an intruder attempting to open the door with tremendous force and a consistent pulling of the doorknob, in the direction it would have been opened from before. Both of them had witnessed this yet couldn't explain it. After the activity subsided and they got the courage to investigate, no one was found to be on the other side of the closed-off bathroom, nor were there any signs of a break-in.

Several years later, my mother called me to relay some unfortunate news. The TV in the living room (where they had spent many hours in front of) finally called it quits. Rick loved that TV because it had been with him a number of years. It remained neatly housed inside a solidly constructed cabinet, which had become a permanent staple of the living room. The cabinet was over twenty years old and had traveled with him after his first marriage into his current house, so one might imagine there was already some emotional attachment to the unit. It also contained a five-disc DVD player, a VCR player, a cassette deck, a stereo receiver, numerous videocassettes and discs—and on top of all that—the unit would proudly display his collection of miniature villages and Christmas decorations. It was something that the rest of the room had been designed around.

Margie is a person that embraces the latest and greatest technology and was more than happy to upgrade everything, yet as a faithful wife, she supported her husband's decision to keep the entertainment center in place until that fateful day of doom for the TV set. Even though they were both ready for a more modern setup, it was not a task Rick necessarily looked forward to. The cleanup and preparation required him to revisit and bid farewell to numerous fond memories attached to items that had been buried underneath a sea of dust-covered cables long forgotten to the dark reaches of cabinet space.

When the space had been cleared, I was sent a photo of the empty void that remained in the shadow of its former glory. As the television and entertainment center were moved outside to the trash, Rick retreated to his sanctuary and work station in the basement—an area of familiarity and refuge where he could escape the loss and contemplate, even if just momentarily. Plus, there was another vintage TV set there nestled among more collectibles and historical treasures of his.

Margie was on the second floor watching shows on another set when suddenly a message came overtop the TV screen to state that service had been interrupted and to check cable connections or call the service provider. There was no way she was going to call the provider and spend hours on the phone, so she went to the basement to see if Rick had been having any issues with his TV. He indicated there had not been a single interruption, which didn't make sense to her since all of the television sets in the house were connected to the same cable provider.

So she did what the on-screen prompt had suggested, disconnecting and reconnecting various wires, but it didn't seem to help. She repeated the same process of disconnecting and reconnecting, yet the on-screen prompt remained. When the TV was turned off then back on again, only the channel indicator displayed on the screen. She pressed the channel up and down buttons randomly and the TV was suddenly back to its normal operation.

Margie resumed watching her programs, then the ceiling light flipped on and off three times. This has become a code that her and Rick do to signal to each other instead of shouting up and down the stairs. After recognizing the indicator, she called down to Rick to come up, but there was no response. She waited a moment then called back down again—and again no response. She went to the top of the stairs to call down to him a third time, but he wasn't there. Confused, she went downstairs to the basement and saw him relaxed in his chair and watching TV. She asked him again if he had experienced any strange electricity malfunctions, but everything had been perfectly normal for him.

My mother assumed that their invisible house guest from the sunroom renovations had returned. I thought about the possibility, but based on the emotional state Rick had been in at the moment, I thought of something else. Maybe this was not a ghost by the classic definition of the sense, but rather a ghosted psychic impression of another Rick from another point in time/space. Perhaps it was fueled by the mentality of his stressful state and triggered by this sudden "tragedy" and removal of the broken equipment he had grown attached to.

The presence had directly affected Margie but left Rick alone. On other occasions around this same time, she heard movement coming up the steps, along with the signature sound of Rick's ankle cracking, yet when the sound reached the top of the stairs, there was no one there. Of course, some might argue all of this could've merely been a combination of technical anomalies, house resettling, and general coincidences.

Not Exactly a Way to Impress People

I've heard from many women that they are lucky not to be involved with someone like me. Living with a researcher or investigator into bizarre phenomena presents a different kind of challenge. And I should know. When we were together Carrie had to experience many strange things that I'm sure she would've rather not dealt with. At the same time, I think it also brought about a great comfort. Since a crippling fear of the invisible was absent in me, I was the go-to guy for all sorts of visible presences—

things like spiders and bugs and other creepy-crawlies that prowl around in the darkness.

I once consulted Shannon and Russ—two newlyweds committed to each other, but not to the uninvited third wheel they thought moved in with them to their new home. Russ had a keen interest in the paranormal and had considered joining my investigative group at the time. Shannon however, was quite the opposite. Yet both had had their fair share of independent, inexplicable circumstances that they were intrigued by. When I presented the opportunity for Russ to look at joining a paranormal group as a way to understand his own history with high strangeness, Shannon was hesitant.

"But what if you bring something home with you?" she asked her husband with concern. I explained that it was always a possibility, but a highly unlikely one given the relatively "safe" cases I had new investigators go on and the necessary protocols taken to minimize that risk. Shannon was still apprehensive about the whole affair and who could blame her?

I added, "Well, it's something that the both of you have to agree to. It would be unfair for just one of you to pursue this subject if the other wasn't completely supportive of it."

I give Carrie the utmost credit in that regard. Although she had wanted to have nothing to do with my interest in the topic overall, she had always been supportive of my pursuit of it. However, that support was tested several times, like the morning following an investigation when the gloves in her purse disappeared, only to rematerialize back inside her purse moments later. After that one she told me I had better find a ghost maid to clean the house instead.

The plethora of paranormal television shows has certainly made it easier to bring up this topic around others. And even though great numbers of paranormal investigators are not particularly fond of the attention these shows have brought to the field, or more specifically, the inexperienced amateurs they seem to encourage, we really owe these forums more than that. They have helped people who are experiencing activity to come forward and talk about it more comfortably. However, I still have to be careful in how I bring up this topic to those that I speak with. In some cases, it has cost me potential friendships, or caused irreversible damage to existing ones. As glamorous as we tend to think our duties are as paranormal researchers and investigators alike, it's certainly not a way to impress those who don't share our same passions, let alone understand them.

One such example took place during a wedding rehearsal dinner for close friends of mine. I was introduced to several of the bridesmaids and had captivated these women with the stories and situations I found myself in through the years, excluding all the paranormal ones. At one point in the evening, the groom interrupted our conversation to ask, "So, did you tell them about what you do?"

I replied, "Oh with screenwriting? Of course! I have to keep practicing my pitch to strangers before I attempt Hollywood, you know."

But inside I knew exactly what the groom meant and hoped he wouldn't bring it up. I knew the blessings and the curses being involved in the field can bring, especially in attempting to make new friends and fit in.

"No, I mean your other job," he added. "You know…the GHOST HUNTING."

The groom's words seemed to emerge in slow motion, like ectoplasmic goo, as I saw the faces on some of the women turn as white as ghosts.

What I'm continually reminded of is that there are some people who are frightened immediately by the topic and want to have nothing to do with it. And then there are others who want to keep pushing the envelope to find out if the whole topic even has merit to begin with. The latter of which usually regret it once I begin to relay some of my more harrowing encounters. (Thankfully, that's not you or else you wouldn't have picked up this book to begin with.)

A couple of the bridesmaids were of that latter, curious kind. So, I started telling them about how monotonous, boring and uneventful investigations can be, trying to downplay the whole affair. After all, I was trying to make friends for the wedding, not repel them. We still had a whole ceremony to endure the next day and standing around for six plus hours with the awkwardness of being the creepy, resident ghost hunter everybody avoids was less than desirable. But one specific woman didn't care about all that. She wanted to hear the good stuff—the scary stuff. So, after refusing no for an answer, I began to dish her the darkness. The stuff Hollywood usually turns into films.

We might as well have been in the woods sitting around some campfire roasting marshmallows, because by the time the night had ended, not even a marshmallow could compare to how white this woman turned. In fact, I had heard later that she and the other bridesmaids were so terrified to go to sleep later that night that they spent most of it holed up together in one hotel room clutching each other for dear life. At the wedding, most of the bridal party wouldn't speak to me longer than a couple of minutes at most. They were probably so scared that I might somehow send a ghost home with them that night instead of a drunken wedding attendee.

At this point, I started to reevaluate what my main purpose is in this field. I no longer wanted to focus primarily on investigations, so much as I wanted to take the fear out of the entire subject. Since then, I've been able to help dispel some of the preconceived notions from what Hollywood showcases, and present the more accurate aspects to several people I've spoken with.

I continue to initiate conversations with strangers, even though some of them tend to go nowhere—particularly those with drunken people at bars or extreme fundamentalists in religious circles. I never know whom I'll meet on this journey and what strange story they might have to share. Lots of strange events are never formally reported to investigative groups or research organizations, so until we inquire, we'll never know.

Striking up a conversation with someone who has something to add can be one of the more rewarding aspects. On the contrary, I've lost many a so-called friend because of my involvement with it as well.

"What I have seen with my own eyes and my own experiences seems to be multidimensional or para-physical more than it seems to be physical."[41]

– Brad Steiger

41 *Dreamland.* Premiere Radio Networks. 08 Oct. 1995.

Dangers of Paranormal Research

There are risks and rewards associated with any line of work. For some, the risks help define who they are and shape what they become.

For the active investigator, proper care is needed not just physically, but mentally, emotionally, and spiritually as well in order to maintain the right attitude and careful approach to the phenomena. When I was actively involved with investigating, peculiar events would occur, and presences would sometimes appear when I'd least expect it. Through some rather unsettling experiences, I realized the phenomenon is much bigger than any one of us, even though we'd like to think otherwise. We are naïve to believe that we have much control over the spectrum, if any at all.

If you are going to get involved with this subject, or simply just take an active interest in it, be aware. Something out there pulling the strings enjoys implementing trickery and deceit to deter those from attempting to understand its true nature. We need to be mindful of these forces, which can have a powerful effect on us in more ways than we realize.

When an individual becomes deeply involved in this research, their involvement can be met with a string of seemingly bad luck or occurrences that take a bizarre turn for the worst. Researchers like Nick Redfern have explored this concept in what's referred to as *psychic backlash*.[42] This is when the phenomenon appears to realize that it's being observed and responds in a detrimental manner. John Keel dealt with this concept when he was

---

42 Redfern, Nick. "The Hazards of Psychic Backlash." *Mysterious Universe*. 8th Kind Pty Ltd. 06 Dec. 2013. Web. 08 May 2017. http://mysteriousuniverse.org/2013/12/the-hazards-of-psychic-backlash

involved with the strange events in and around the Point Pleasant, WV region, chronicled in his book, *The Mothman Prophecies.* The effect was also intense enough to thwart UFO researcher Albert K. Bender at the height of his career after a run-in with three mysterious men, who later formed the basis of the modern-era Men in Black reports, outlined in his book, *Flying Saucers and the Three Men.*

When Conditions Are Ripe

The world of the unexplained is no doubt a fascinating one, but it is not one to be studied carelessly. Although it is unlikely to ever experience the extreme nature of being under the metaphysical microscope, we shouldn't underestimate its ability, should we find ourselves in a high strangeness storm of parapsychological precipitation. In April 2014, a paranormal convention called *Phenomacon* took place in Gettysburg, Pennsylvania. The three-day event was held at the Eisenhower Hotel—a reportedly known haunted location—but then again, it's Gettysburg; what part of it isn't haunted? An extensive list of speakers lined the lecture halls, which included various talks on all angles of paranormal research.

Although I did not attend the entire weekend, I was fortunate enough to sit in on a few of the lectures on Saturday, including one with radio talk show host Dave Schrader on thought-forms, which I wish I had recorded. There have only been a couple of lectures that have left lasting impressions on me and that one certainly did.

It was the first big paranormal conference I ever attended. With all due respect to the paranormal field, I am more drawn to the ufology conferences, as they tend to be more focused on findings from studies and case reports and less on the fan followings that much of the popular paranormal entertainment attracts. And even though there can be a fine line separating ghostly experiences from UFO sightings, there is clearly a vast difference in how each genre's events are structured in terms of style and attendance.

For the most part, I was impressed with Phenomacon. The event organizers achieved the right mix in attracting both serious researchers and paranormal enthusiasts alike. The lectures made for an enriching experience and the ideal environment for meeting people and making new friendships with those sharing similar interests.

Rosalyn Lewis (formerly Rosalyn Bown), a now lifelong friend that I first met there, tipped me off about a set of curious events that took place behind the scenes of the event, and even during it. As usual, the most exciting moments happen when they are least expected.

On Friday, the day before I had arrived, there happened to be a panel discussion on violent hauntings, with the likes of the Perrons, the Pickmans, Carmen Reed, Bill Bean, Chris Dedman, and Jeff Leeper. To those of you not familiar with these individuals, they are all people that have either encountered negative hauntings in their life or have helped those out in dealing with such. During the discussion, even the audience witnessed strange events, which Carmen Reed later elaborated and confirmed to me.

Carmen explained that whenever she does a speaking engagement, she would enter the room first, long before anyone arrives, in order to cleanse it of any negative energy. However, before this particular lecture at Phenomacon, she was unable to do so. As a result, she quickly picked up on feelings of anguish right from the beginning. She sensed there was a presence in the room, even feeling it in the form of a slight wind whirling around when she sat down.[43]

The audience seemed engaged in the topics that were discussed, but Carmen could sense tension on the panel and an increased agitation brewing in the air. It was at a point when the moderator asked the panel how they felt about Ed and Lorraine Warren conducting séances in their homes that a tall tree to the right of the stage blew over. There were also strange knocks on the side door and something flying around like paper, according to the reports. At one point, Carmen told the audience just to ignore the presence and give it no recognition. A wise suggestion as these things seem to have the ability to grow in power once they are acknowledged.[44]

It doesn't surprise me that something like this would occur, especially in a haunted locale with haunted people and haunted enthusiasts. It's the perfect psychic super storm of energies and emotions all coming together and charging up the environment. And it didn't stop just there, either.

Attendee Larissa Mrykalo experienced one such incident, which took place in her bedroom suite of the Eisenhower. She was located next to the indoor pool on the first floor. Staying in there for two nights, Larissa sensed a level of uneasiness that another friend of hers felt manifest into the form of an invisible entity sitting on the bed and touching her back.

---

43 Reed, Carmen. Interview conducted via electronic messaging. 17 Apr. 2014.

44 Reed, Carmen. Interview conducted via electronic messaging. 17 Apr. 2014.

The experience would be enough to convince that friend to stay somewhere else the following morning.[45]

Now I don't claim to be a Feng Shui expert, but the first thing I noticed upon entering her room was the absence of windows to the outside, no mirrors on the walls, cramped quarters and a décor reminiscent of something out of the 1970s. Aside from a prison of lousy wallpaper, could the energy have somehow become trapped without an easy way to escape?

The activity continued for Larissa and a different roommate on night two after the first roommate relocated somewhere else. These two women witnessed a series of strange knocking that seemed to respond to their commands. Whatever was in there with them—residual, intelligent or something else—it was no doubt unwelcomed.

Another report of strange activity experienced by some of the Phenomacon attendees was what was described as "waves of negative energy" throughout certain areas of the conference rooms. This seems to be contrary to what one would expect amidst such a positive group of paranormal enthusiasts. But regardless, it appeared to have happened to at least three others that weekend, according to comments posted to the Phenomacon Facebook page.

One attendee recalled a peculiar incident with another friend in the grand ballroom...

> *"We were walking and in conversation when we looked at each other at the very same time, twice, because we walked through intense waves of energy that nearly stopped us in our tracks. The energy was kind of hard to shake. When I walked back through the same area an hour or so later, the air felt normal and I didn't feel anything else there the rest of the weekend."*[46]

Another attendee recalled pockets of energy in the vendor room that particularly stood out for them...

---

45 Mrykalo, Larissa. Personal interview conducted 12 Apr. 2014.

46 "Several people experienced unexpected/unsolicited paranormal experiences... what was yours?" *Phenomenology/Phenom Events.* 14 Apr. 2014. Excerpt of a comment left on 19 Apr. 2014, 11:48 a.m. by Chrisy Milliken. https://www.facebook.com/PhenomEvents/posts/616047241810271

"I got a harsh wave of negative energy come at me near a booth in vendor's area that is never fun, but helps me learn how to fight it off. This was the most direct and intense feeling yet."[47]

And another, like Larissa, experienced something that also joined them in their hotel room on the property…

"Lots of random tapping/knocking sounds, heavy feelings in certain areas, the feeling of being watched...oh and something jumping on my bed while touching my back. So different from last year! Never a dull moment."[48]

But what was causing all this intense energy—some sort of mass hysteria? One can only speculate. Carmen said that whenever she gets very involved in discussing the events surrounding her own haunting (chronicled in the 2009 film *The Haunting in Connecticut),* bizarre things would also take place as a result. In response, she takes every precaution for the safety of those who come to listen to her.[49]

Maybe speakers at paranormal conferences kick up activity in such a way and not even know it. Or maybe the intense focal energy from the audience helps to foster it. Larissa summed it up best by saying— "The energy gets really odd at the events. Think about combining an already notoriously haunted area with all of those psychics and mediums. It's like the big Twinkie in *Ghostbusters!*"[50]

47 "Several people experienced unexpected/unsolicited paranormal experiences… what was yours?" *Phenomenology/Phenom Events.* 14 Apr. 2014. Excerpt of a comment left on 14 Apr. 2014, 11:47 a.m. by Melanie Rogers. https://www.facebook.com/PhenomEvents/posts/616047241810271

48 "Several people experienced unexpected/unsolicited paranormal experiences… what was yours?" *Phenomenology/Phenom Events.* 14 Apr. 2014. Excerpt of a comment left on 14 Apr. 2014, 10:44 a.m. by Nowal Massari. https://www.facebook.com/PhenomEvents/posts/616047241810271

49 Reed, Carmen. Interview conducted via electronic messaging. 19 Apr. 2014.

50 Mrykalo, Larissa. Correspondences conducted via electronic messaging. 13 Apr. 2014.

Being Scared and Becoming Scarred

Some enthusiasts think it would be awesome to live in a haunted house. But those that actually do live in them say the opposite. Behind the veil of para-popularity there exists a darker and more troubling scenario that few can even imagine. Fewer still truly understand how much this can take a toll on—or even destroy—lives in the process. These people are often referred to as haunting survivors. One such survivor is a man I'll refer to as "Lawrence Miller." Due to the nature of his profession and the long-term troubling effects of his ordeal, he asked that I preserve his true identity and his family's for the time being.[51]

Lawrence is a Houston, Texas IT consultant by day and member of a paranormal team by night. Before he became an active investigator, the topic of ghosts wasn't something he had been seeking out. For some, it doesn't really matter where you're coming from on the debate; the paranormal seeks you, regardless. And for this man, it was something that would ultimately send his world into a completely different direction.

In the spring of 2008, Lawrence accepted a promising job offer in Charleston, South Carolina after deciding that his career in Houston was going nowhere. Charleston presented a fresh start with a rich culture, fine cuisine, and easy ocean access for his wife, "Shoshana" and twelve-year old daughter, "Ruth." Even seemingly little things like the pollen count, was ideal for his daughter, who struggled with asthma on a daily basis. For the Miller family, it was the perfect environment to flock to.

---

51 "Miller, Lawrence." Phone interview. 06 Sept. 2014.

However, in the blink of an eye, everything suddenly went left. The company rescinded their offer at the last minute. The Millers had their heart and mind set on the area and Lawrence knew he didn't want to go back to Houston. He needed to find another job, and fast. Fortunately, he stumbled upon an IT security position at a major health group in Columbia. It wasn't Charleston, but at least it was in the same state. While he worked for this new company, his family remained in Texas while he took up short-term residence at a nearby hotel in town. The plan being that once he could find a more permanent residence in the area, the rest of his family would rejoin him.

It wasn't long after Lawrence had been working in Columbia that he realized the area was not quite what he had expected. The environment there was less than ideal. Separated from his family, combined with the long work hours, quickly took its toll on him. The once fantastic opportunity the Miller family had been looking forward to now was rapidly eroding.

But things started looking up after Lawrence discovered a house for sale, only nine minutes from his current company. The property was situated within a small cul-de-sac community and adjacent to a quiet golf course. It was a nice location to move his family into. The house was a stereotypical split-level suburban structure. It was built in the eighties, included a pool, and for the price, was an offer too good to pass up on. The previous owners had been a young married couple—the husband in banking, the wife in real estate. The couple had explained that they were selling the house to move across town to an area with a better commute.

However, Lawrence thought that there weren't any other places in Columbia, at least in those two professions, which took longer than twenty minutes to get to. Was it really a commute issue? Perhaps it was because the couple had recently become new parents and needed additional room to expand. After all, they had only owned the house for about two years.

Either way, it wasn't something Lawrence thought much of. He put an offer on the property and the sale quickly went through. He moved into the house only a few weeks before his family arrived to get acquainted with the property.

In those first few days, there was nothing out of the ordinary, aside from the usual odd sounds attributed to normal house settling. One of the peculiar things Lawrence took note of was that the sellers had left behind lots of little random things. Items like baby toys and hardware tools along with home improvement projects that had been started, but never finished.

And of those projects, there were even some that hadn't been initiated by the previous sellers—but rather by the occupants before them. Still, it wasn't enough to distract Lawrence from welcoming his own family once they arrived.

After moving in, his wife Shoshana picked up on a bad feeling about the property. Unlike Lawrence, she had always been spiritually in-touch because of her Native American upbringing. Having been partially raised on a reservation, she spent most of her childhood immersed in the more mystical aspects of the culture and was no stranger to the strange. Even though Lawrence hadn't been "tuned in to that sort of thing," there was an unrelated incident he recalled as a child, in which he regularly saw the apparition of a human seated in a chair at a neighbor's house. Although he never felt threatened by the presence, he was strangely comforted by it.

Back at their new house, the Millers' next-door neighbors took a peculiar interest in the property. They wouldn't reveal anything specific, but admitted they had suspicions something strange had been taking place there: several people would move in then vacate shortly thereafter. In an attempt to uncover history or potential clues for the high turnover rate, Lawrence reached out to the previous couple that had sold him the property, but they ignored him. The other neighbors weren't much help, either. At the middle school where their daughter Ruth had enrolled, there was a teacher who had lived in the house when it was first built. She was concerned to hear that Ruth moved in, but never elaborated on the reason why.

Inside the house, the walls were originally painted an ugly yellow—or more eloquently explained as a "pus yellow." But that was an easy fix for professional painters hired to cover it up. A calming cappuccino gray was selected for the living and dining rooms, complimenting a deep maroon for the master bedroom. But even with three coats of the gray paint and six coats of the red, the ugly yellow still bled through. Soon after, red paint began to leak out of the walls in other parts of their home.

Then there was the sticky residue everywhere. For the Millers, mopping the linoleum floors each day didn't seem to make much of a difference. A tacky feel still remained on virtually every surface of the house. They found themselves in a constant battle of cleaning, but to no avail.

At one point, a small valve in the refrigerator broke that was attached to the ice maker. Since the valve was situated inside the wall, it flooded both the wall and all of the floors. Because of this, they decided to have brand new linoleum installed throughout the downstairs, along with hardwood in some areas. If anything, they hoped it was a blessing in disguise that would allow them to finally conquer the stickiness issue once and for all. Yet to their dismay, they discovered the new flooring had also succumbed to the strange stickiness!

Then came the eerie visual manifestations…

The first encounter appeared to Lawrence in the form of a Revolutionary War-era soldier. Contrary to the public perception that ghosts only come out at night, this apparition made its way from room to room at any time of day or night, and without acknowledgement of anything, nor anyone. Now that alone is strange enough, especially with such regularity as Lawrence claimed to have seen it, but not nearly as odd as what he would witness soon after.

First in the periphery, then later directly in front of him, he started to see little creatures. They had strong physical characteristics similar to the imps and dwarves of popular folklore. As he put it, "There were different ones. There was one that was kind of like about four feet tall, whitish... tightness like an exoskeleton kind of thing; big, bulgy eyes. The main one was about three feet tall, reddish orange; had a face with a bulbous nose. Big eyes with a face that looked like a mask, but it wasn't a mask—it was his face. They had long fingers. There were other ones that we saw less frequently."[52]

But were these demons instead? If so, Lawrence certainly didn't want to identify or name them as such. In fact, when I inquired into that particular aspect, it was met with hesitation— "That theory I have come up with," is all he would say.[53]

Ruth said she would frequently hear disembodied whispers in her bedroom. Lawrence decided to stay with her in her bedroom one night to see if he could witness it himself. Sure enough, he did, so he moved his daughter into another room over the garage, complete with her very own bathroom suite. It was a pretty grand deal for a teenage girl really, and one that Lawrence hoped would eventually distract her from anything else that took place later on in the rest of the house. It was the one thing he wished for that actually came true.

52 "Miller, Lawrence." Phone interview. 06 Sept. 2014.

53 "Miller, Lawrence." Phone interview. 06 Sept. 2014.

Since the new bedroom had not been part of the original construction, Lawrence theorized this acted as a sort of sanctuary from the rest of the activity. Even their cats took up residence in that room during the day when the rest of the house was empty. For whatever reason, they would completely avoid the master bedroom—the place where most of the activity would later manifest.

There came a point for Lawrence that apparently being the only one that actually saw these things weighed heavy on his mental state. After all, no one else had mentioned it, so he merely kept it to himself. The possibility he could have been losing his mind all along led him to turn to alcohol as a coping mechanism, for he discovered that if he drank enough, they would no longer appear.

Whatever you may be thinking about Lawrence's character up until this point is completely understandable. On the surface, it appears to be the story of a man who is slowly unraveling and becoming an alcoholic. But let's consider this scenario in terms of the unnatural, inhuman, or maybe even demonic. The standard modus operandi of such forces (if we are to consider that a possibility in this case) is to destroy humanity—whether through mental, emotional, physical, or any combination of such. What better way to achieve that than to play off of the emotions of a man already stressed out? Perhaps the eventual goal of the creatures was to further encourage him to destroy himself—and worse yet, his family—in the process.

Division, especially within the home, is one of the more common tactics in order to lead to isolation of the target. This allows the targeted individual to become vulnerable to the oppression stage, one of the three main stages of demonic activity.[54] And in Lawrence's case, that is exactly what began to take place. It wasn't long before he and his wife started to drift apart. He worked long hours each day and rarely got a restful sleep after as the creatures in the house continued to keep him up. He soon became irritated, upset, distant and depressed.

At that time, Shoshana had been prescribed Ambien to help combat a chronic insomniac condition, which didn't fare well with Lawrence, who was in a drunken stupor most of the time. Combine this with the added stress of the supernatural and it's not exactly the ideal concoction for a

---

54 Sarchie, Ralph and Lisa Collier Cool. "Caught by the Occult." *Deliver Us From Evil: A New York City Cop Investigates the Supernatural.* Kindle ed., St. Martin's Griffin, 2014. pg. 147.

great family dynamic. Plus, up until that point he still hadn't told anyone about the visions, either. He thought he was slowly losing a grip on reality and considered that the creatures were nothing more than mere delusions. The only problem was that the so-called delusions were becoming more and more vivid each day. And he had to drink more and more just to escape them.

One evening, Lawrence ventured to the outdoor deck for a smoke, where he observed three children playing a ring-around-the-rosy type game in the backyard. He thought it was odd, given that their property was fenced in. But as he continued to watch them dance across his yard, then across his pool, they eventually just faded out around the corner of the house. This left him dumbfounded. He thought, "Had I just witnessed little kids walk across water then vanish into thin air?"[55]

Shoshana soon stopped taking the Ambien after an expensive order was placed online unknowingly and attributed to her "sleep-shopping." The insomnia quickly returned, so she would often spend the entire night completely awake. One morning, just before Lawrence's alarm went off, she woke him to relate an experience she had while he had been asleep. Apparently, a strange looking creature had kept its eyes intently on her from the side of the bed while she was on her laptop.

Could this have been a mere hallucination resulting from lack of sleep? Perhaps. That is until she described in detail the exact same creature Lawrence had seen. He was both stunned and relieved that these things hadn't been just a figment of his imagination. After Shoshana became aware of the creatures, she also started to see the ghostly soldier.

Ruth heard them talking about the strange events and wanted to see the activity herself, so she could be part of it. But they never showed themselves to her for some reason. It appeared that it was only Lawrence and Shoshana that the phenomena latched on to. In demonology, I've heard that typically the activity will torment the youngest members of the family, but in this case that wasn't evident. Between the two adults there was enough high strangeness. Hell-bent on wearing them down little by little, it decided to attack them next with electronic annoyances.

Various digital devices malfunctioned what seemed like every day. DVD players had to be continuously replaced. Two televisions went haywire. Six wireless routers stopped working. Computer motherboards abruptly malfunctioned. The Millers didn't even know refrigerators had

55 "Miller, Lawrence." Phone interview. 06 Sept. 2014.

motherboards until that too went kaput. All of the electronics in the house had been shorted out, so an electrician was called in to inspect the wiring.

For the most part, the electrician thought the wiring looked good, but the configuration was a little odd. He explained that the wires ran in such a way that was contrary to other houses. There were wires running in the middle of walls, along the ground and through the roof in an atypical pattern. The electrician wasn't even sure it was up to code, but said it wasn't broken enough to really worry about. What it did do however was create high electrical fields around everything.

It is believed by paranormal investigators that prolonged exposure to high electromagnetic fields (EMF) can cause adverse effects such as uneasiness, excitability, stress, paranoia, nausea and even hallucinations to those sensitive to pick up on them. There might even be a connection between high EMFs and reportedly haunted locations as the direct culprit in a lot of the perceived activity.

Because Lawrence's profession required him to occasionally work at home, and often with expensive equipment, he wanted to make sure the wiring problem was solved once and for all. The danger in his company's equipment getting destroyed was not something he wanted to be responsible for. So, the power company was called out to conduct some initial tests on the property. They discovered that there were unexplained power surges coming in to the house. But the surges weren't the result of hard-wired power lines coming from the street to the property. Instead, the junction was made with a random stack of washers. They concluded it was the probable cause for the mysterious surges and removed them promptly to install actual wiring in its place.

"Why wasn't that caught with the initial home inspection, along with lots of other issues, before he purchased the property?" Lawrence thought.

As the electricians analyze the new flow of power to the house, they noticed that there was still something that drew an enormous spike of power to the house at exactly ten-minute intervals. They went to each part of the property, turning various items off in an attempt to pinpoint the source. Even then, they still could not determine where exactly the power surges originated. They finally decided to just shut off the master breaker, but even without any power to the house, the mystery spike was still present.

After they were unable to explain the cause of the phantom power surges, one of the electricians turned to Lawrence and said, "Look, I don't know what is going on here, but maybe your place is haunted or something." The other electrician agreed with his joke. But it didn't seem like the first guy had made a joke. In fact, he was dead serious in his expression. It was the first time all day that the electrician had been serious about anything, according to Lawrence. He even looked somewhat frightened to consider the unexplained pockets of energy he had also come across earlier in the day with his EMF detector.

Smudging is a technique that uses a bundle of dry herbs (such as sage) usually bound into a tight bundle and then burned. The carrier of the smudging stick walks from room to room waving the bundle through the air in an attempt to "push out" the negative energy from a place. This is called clearing or cleansing a room. The Millers decided they would attempt to cleanse their house with this ancient Native American ritual, since all else had presumably failed.

It is important to note the preparation that goes into such a technique. It requires a level of spiritual confidence to work properly, and according to Lawrence, "you can't half ass."[56] What ends up usually occurring, especially with those who perform the cleansing ritual on their own without proper instruction, is it makes things even worse. Lawrence admitted that he didn't have much faith that the smudging technique would be all that effective—and he was right. Things became a lot worse after that.

The electronic malfunctions continued, visual manifestation became more frequent, and soon the unseen physical attacks began. One of the cats fell unexpectedly ill and died. Another dislocated its shoulder, so it was kept in a crate in the master bedroom where they could keep an eye on it. Though they didn't suspect any supernatural forces were at play in the injury, there was a situation with the crate itself, which would play into another occurrence later on.

When Shoshana's computer broke, they decided to take it to the nearest service center—an Apple facility located in Charlotte, about ninety minutes away. When they got back, they found that the items they had put on top of the cat crate were resting neatly alongside it. As for the cat, it was covered in food and water from head to tail. Something had visibly shaken it up, but what? After that event, the cat refused to ever go back in the crate ever again. The crate itself remained in the bedroom but sat empty.

On another evening, Lawrence had quickly fallen asleep in the bed with Shoshana next to him, on her laptop. He felt something scamper

56 "Miller, Lawrence." Phone interview. 06 Sept. 2014.

quickly across him on the bed but thought it was probably one of the cats. However, he was immediately awoken by the blood-curdling scream of Shoshana seconds later. She explained that a white bony creature had crawled across her, sat on her chest and had started to play with her face with its long, pointy fingers. The creature just stared at her while doing so, preventing her from being able to take in breaths, then simply vanished. She couldn't go back to sleep after that one. You wouldn't, either.

After the horrific encounter, Shoshana took to sleeping from sunrise to mid-afternoons in the downstairs living room and staying up all night watching infomercials out of fear that one of the creatures might attack. Late at night in the reflection of the patio door glass, she would see movement take place behind her—things walking back and forth across the room or jumping in order to get her attention. After getting used to the shenanigans, her reaction was nonchalant, simply walking over to close the curtains so she didn't notice the reflections anymore.

But the entities became more vigorous in an attempt to get her attention, according to Lawrence. At that point, the family entertained the thought of moving out of the house. Lawrence made arrangements to work from home for the remainder of his time with the company while simultaneously packing up for the potential move back to Texas, should the activity continue.

One final incident was enough to push them out once and for all...

Late one night, as the two of them were in bed, they heard a persistent clicking sound coming from the latch on the crate. It was enough to get Shoshana to retreat back downstairs to her "safe zone" out of sheer frustration. Meanwhile, Lawrence remained in the bed by himself, able to ignore the clicking, as it resembled a metronome to lull him back asleep with relative ease.

Then unexpectedly, a red bulbous creature jumped up on the bed, scampered across his body and sprawled itself across Lawrence's head to completely cover his face. Lawrence struggled to breathe as the creature pinned down his arms in an attempt to suffocate him. Lawrence was very much awake at that point because he said he could feel a heavy weight sitting on his entire head.[57]

---

57 "Miller, Lawrence." Phone interview. 06 Sept. 2014.

In an attempt to fight for his life, Lawrence freed his right arm and began to assault the creature with a barrage of blind punching. He could feel flesh on bone as his fist connected with the creature's ribs and spine. There was something quite tangible that he felt in the moment, along with the physical sound his fist made upon repeatedly connecting with the creature's body.

Had Lawrence been dreaming? If it had been a dream and this thing did not exist, then he certainly would have been slugging himself in the face and would have the marks to prove it. Could it have been one of his cats? If that were the case, he said he would've totally killed the cat because of the sheer force he had been putting into each blow.

After a few moments of what seemed like an eternity, the creature scurried off, and air filled his lungs once again. It was enough to allow him to scream for Shoshana. They decided they would leave the house as soon as possible after that—two days later, to be exact.

"Whatever didn't fit in the U-Haul, we left," Lawrence explained.[58]

Between this final incident and the Millers vacating the property, no further activity took place. And it never followed them back to Texas, either. I can't help but think that if this were something typically demonic by classic definition, it might have followed them, no matter where they went. Perhaps these creatures were just defending their territory against outside visitors. One can only speculate.

The Millers soon settled back in the Houston area. Lawrence and Shoshana divorced shortly after as a result of the stress from the ordeal and aftermath. It not only broke them emotionally, but financially as well. If it was demonic, it certainly succeeded in the division part.

Since the Millers left, the house has been sold twice. Maybe again, by the time you read this. Later research by Lawrence uncovered that nobody ever stayed in the house longer than two years. His family was there for two and a half. If the whole thing were just a hallucination, then why would so many people move out after such a short amount of time?

Lawrence was officially diagnosed with post-traumatic stress disorder (PTSD) as a result of the final event that took place in the house. To this day, he seeks treatment to cope with it. His latest therapist, who is not a "ghost guy" by any means, had told him that if what he had experienced were in fact, a hallucination, it wouldn't have caused the lasting damage on his brain to the extent of PTSD. He further explained that there is no way

58 "Miller, Lawrence." Phone interview. 06 Sept. 2014.

for one's own hallucination to leave effects like this on the human psyche without it being very much real.

Lawrence is still uncomfortable talking about the events that took place there. But in a way, it's also therapeutic to confront them and understand that there are others that can relate to his ordeal. Events like his can be very frightening for anyone not expecting it. Investigators and researchers need to understand this and make every effort to not just investigate activity, but also help a haunting survivor seek treatment through the effects of it afterwards. Whether or not you believe Lawrence's story to be true, it is undeniable that something very real took place and scarred him. Even though it is no longer present within his own home, whatever took place in that house affected him on a level that will probably haunt him forever.

The incident itself does have a redeeming aspect, though. It prompted Lawrence to look for a paranormal group in Texas that could offer help to those like him who were going through the same thing. Because of his Jewish faith, it was difficult for his family to find a temple or rabbi that dealt in that topic, let alone even discuss it. He even tried to seek the help of a Catholic priest, but the priest told him that his presence wouldn't have any effect because of his conflicting religious views.

Lawrence inked a "Seal of Solomon" tattoo on his chest a few years later to protect him from anything negative. In Jewish culture, the seal references a supposed magic ring that was given to King Solomon to possess power in commanding demons. There are a few different stories in regard to its origin, but the general symbol is supposed to exhibit overall protective qualities.

After the decision to get the tattoo, Lawrence's nightmares of the incident have stopped. He believes it made a difference, much to the dismay of his investigative group, who hasn't had any significant paranormal experiences since then. In fact, they'll probably try to get rid of him for ruining all the fun. But then again, for those that have actually lived through it, dealing with these forces can be anything but *fun*.

Threats from a Distance

It's one thing to be harassed by something you can physically see; yet it is an entirely different matter when it remains in the vicinity of the sight unseen.

Maybe it's this lack of physicality, or the seeming defiance to it, that generally turn people off to UFO research. Even though parapsychology can also be bathed in darkness, people seem to be more disturbed by the occupants behind the UFOs, instead of the UFOs themselves. Whatever is behind them operates without a clear motive—an aspect that does not sit well with most logical people.

Even though we'd like to think we have a better grasp on why ghosts appear as opposed to the extraterrestrial/ultraterrestrial presence, we should not overlook the notion that both could be emanating from the same source. Perhaps it is the confusing modus operandi displayed by these so-called "aliens," which dissuade paranormal investigators from considering the possibility that they could be interrelated. The lack of a distinct intention by the entities associated with UFOs can be quite unnerving, especially when it comes to their rather intrusive and manipulating characteristics. But these traits also seem to echo the same mannerisms of the paranormal realm, albeit to a lesser degree, or perhaps less apparent to us.

Let's examine the often-contradicting psychological impact the UFO occupants present. Perceptions can range from quite pleasant to quite traumatic, or in some cases, both. Take the Pascagoula, Mississippi case for example. Two men—Charles Hickson (42) and Calvin Parker, Jr. (19)—were both abducted at the same time on October 11, 1973. Hickson viewed his encounter as a rather pleasant experience, yet Parker came away with the complete opposite impression. Hickson saw the same craft in the same area the following year, when a message just suddenly came to him—*they didn't mean any harm.*[59] Yet, Parker wasn't even sure if the creatures he encountered were alien at all, as they could have also been demons in his view.[60]

In the paranormal, ghostly forces can appear as one thing to one person but appear completely different to another who is present during the same experience. For example, one investigator may hear a disembodied voice while a second investigator sees a ball of light at the same location, while a third sees an apparition, but a fourth neither sees nor hears anything at

59 Huneeus, Antonio. "Remembering Charlie Hickson, a rare Pascagoula UFO abduction transcript." *Open Minds.* Open Minds Production. 16 Sept. 2011. Web. 09 May 2017. http://www.openminds.tv/rare-charlie-hickson-transcript-786/12108

60 Amy, Jeff and Stacey Plaisance for the Associated Press. "Calvin Parker tells his story of Pascagoula's famous UFO incident 40 years later." *GulfLive.com.* Alabama Live. 11 Oct. 2013. Web. 09 May 2017. http://blog.gulflive.com/mississippi-press-news/2013/10/calvin_bryant_tells_his_story.html

all! Or in a more mischievous approach, these same paranormal forces can also play a con game of sorts to vulnerable individuals that fall victim to demonic infestation. Demonologist Ralph Sarchie references that angle in his book, *Deliver Us from Evil: A New York City Cop Investigates the Supernatural.* He cites a case where an entity led a family to believe it could help them with the very problem it inflicted by appearing as both a good ghost and a bad ghost, when it was really just the same ghost. It even used a third ghost to pose as the woman's deceased father in order to vouch for its kind intentions and get the family to trust it. But this tactic appears to be nothing more than an open invitation to allow all hell to break loose.[61]

There is a similar case I heard from several New Jersey paranormal investigators that occurred in the home of a Bucks County, Pennsylvania couple. The investigators suspected that demonic forces had pushed a man to commit suicide, and later used his apparition in an attempt to coerce his girlfriend to do the same, along with her new boyfriend. Thankfully the investigators, through the help of an exorcist, stepped in at the right time to help the couple and release them from these oppressive forces.

It's not always the families and individuals that become targets for the phenomenon, but the investigators that try to help them too.

One such example is with accomplished author and researcher Marie D. Jones. To date, she has written on a variety of different topics—from cutting edge science, to the paranormal, ancient history, consciousness and even government mind control. She's experienced harassment issues because of some of them, more recently as a result of her book, *Mind Wars: A History of Mind Control, Surveillance and Social Engineering.* She told me that despite being followed and interrogated by the FBI for her activities, the events that transpired when she became involved with the alien abduction phenomenon in the 1980s and 1990s was unsettling on a much different level.[62]

At that time the abduction phenomenon started to attract widespread media coverage, thanks to researchers like Budd Hopkins, David Jacobs and Whitley Strieber who published their cases and personal encounters. Yet there weren't as many resources for abductees to turn to as there are today. Marie decided to organize a local MUFON group out of another

---

61 Sarchie, Ralph and Lisa Collier Cool. "Nightmares End." *Deliver Us From Evil: A New York City Cop Investigates the Supernatural.* Kindle ed., St. Martin's Griffin, 2014. pp. 25-26.

62 Jones, Marie D. Correspondences via email. 09 May 2017.

woman's home, who she refers to as "Anna" in northern San Diego County, California. Anna, along with her husband, were both abductees.[63]

The two women developed a great friendship as the group flourished. Soon enough, Marie began to receive strange phone calls to her residence. The caller sounded male, yet robotic, almost as if the caller was using a voice-changing gadget. It seemed to know things about her that no one else knew—things like what book was lying on her bed, what she was wearing, or even specific details of what she had done in her twenties.[64] As if that wasn't unsettling enough, the caller also knew when she was home alone, aware that it would creep her out if it called at that time, which it most often did. It insinuated that it could inflict physical harm if it wanted, even though it never actually stated as such, according to the impression she received.[65]

This led Marie to believe that her home was bugged as someone, or something observed her. Since this was before she had Caller ID, she had no way to know who was calling her landline, yet she refrained from alerting the police about it. Eventually the strange calls were too much to bear so she had her telephone number changed.

What Marie notes in Nick Redfern's book, *True Stories of the Real Men in Black (Off the Record!),* is that the caller was less interested in the topic of UFOs, but more interested in her group and what was going on with their abduction research. The caller would often say something like "Your group is familiar with this abductee or that abductee, or with this person or that person," in such a way to let Marie know that it was well-aware of the group's activities.[66]

Meanwhile, Anna also received the strange robotic phone calls, but the harassment went a couple steps further. She and her husband received strange knocks at the door from curious-looking characters and observed people on their property at night that loomed about. They even had their home broken into on occasion. There was a point when Anna's husband

---

63 Redfern, Nick. "Modern Men in Black (Late 1980s and 1990s)." *True Stories of the Real Men in Black (Off the Record!).* The Rosen Publishing Group, 2015, pg. 107.

64 Redfern, Nick. "Modern Men in Black (Late 1980s and 1990s)." *True Stories of the Real Men in Black (Off the Record!).* The Rosen Publishing Group, 2015, pp. 109-110.

65 Redfern, Nick. "Modern Men in Black (Late 1980s and 1990s)." *True Stories of the Real Men in Black (Off the Record!).* The Rosen Publishing Group, 2015, pp. 109-110.

66 Redfern, Nick. "Modern Men in Black (Late 1980s and 1990s)." *True Stories of the Real Men in Black (Off the Record!).* The Rosen Publishing Group, 2015, pg. 110.

went outside with a gun in an attempt to confront the intruders, which he described as appearing like robots—very stiff and stilted, staring without blinking their eyes—yet they still looked human overall.[67]

After the events that transpired, Marie said that she left the group once and for all and never looked back.[68]

Today, Marie writes regularly about UFOs but without issues to the extent she had back then. In her opinion, abduction researchers were a lot more vulnerable than they are now since those involved with the abduction phenomenon were "easy targets," which might explain why the events centered on their group.[69] Today there are a lot more people who claim to be abductees, along with devices and apps that can trace calls, show Caller ID and further document these strange activities.

---

67 Redfern, Nick. "Modern Men in Black (Late 1980s and 1990s)." *True Stories of the Real Men in Black (Off the Record!).* The Rosen Publishing Group, 2015, pp. 107-110.

68 Jones, Marie D. Correspondences via email. 09 May 2017.

69 Jones, Marie D. Correspondences via email. 09 May 2017.

"I will be disappointed if UFOs turn out to be nothing more than spaceships."[70]

– Jacques Vallee

70 "Heretic Among Heretics: Jacques Vallee Interview." *UFO Evidence.* ufoevidence.org. 2011. Web. 25 Jul 2017. http://www.ufoevidence.org/documents/doc839.htm

A Gray World of Little Gray Men

When it comes to the UFO experience there is no black and white approach we can take. It incorporates numerous aspects of the spectrum, ranging from paranormal tie-ins and cryptozoological implications, with the sightings of ships, to contact with the occupants. Interestingly, there seems to be a desire for the UFOs to make themselves known and not known at the same time. The craft will blink in-and-out-of sight leading us to wonder if this is evidence of their extreme maneuverability, or a physical cloaking mechanism, or the ability to jump in-and-out-of our reality, or all of the above and something else altogether? They are tied to our consciousness in some unexplained way too. Witnesses drawn to seeing these things may report a strong urge to go outside just before they suddenly appear. Some even report to be able to summon them simply at will. Abductees commonly report an unexplained connection to the occupants piloting them, which can be recalled as far back as childhood for some.

The beings, or visitors, or extraterrestrials, or ultraterrestrials, or aliens, or entities—whatever we wish to call them—are just like the craft they are associated with. They appear to have a purpose to be seen by some and yet remain elusive to the rest of us. It's almost like these beings want us to be aware of them, but on their terms. Investigative filmmaker Jeremy Corbell puts it best by saying, "They're the ones who are deciding not to reveal themselves, but in these very small, minute and strange ways."[71]

---

71 Corbell, Jeremy. "Extraordinary Beliefs: Series Trailer." *Vimeo.* 24 Feb. 2015. http://vimeo.com/111577536

Could these beings want to reveal themselves, and yet the larger world powers seek to prevent it? This is the usual argument put forth by the conspiracy theorists for a number of reasons. One of those reasons centers on the idea that governments consider the population unable to handle the possibility of intelligent life apart from humans. Advocates for this angle quickly point to the Brookings Report, or the infamous Orson Welles' "*War of the Worlds*" 1938 radio broadcast as further evidence to support it. Some that lean on the suppression conspiracy even more, view it as a form of control that enables the military-industrial complex to utilize E.T. technology for their own purposes, then disseminate it to the populace when it's marketable. Those like Colonel Philip J. Corso have supported this notion as he claimed to have been one of those involved in such a program.[72]

But what if there was another reason why the information was being suppressed, withheld, or even covered-up by the powers that be? Everyone likes to point the finger of disapproval at the government, but maybe the answer isn't that simple to begin with.

Let's consider the events that took place at the now infamous Gorman ranch, a.k.a. Sherman Ranch, a.k.a. Skinwalker Ranch—a hot spot of anomalous activity in northeastern Utah, located around the Uinta Basin near the town of Ballard. The region is a place known for strange UFO activity, but also something much more sinister than just that. It's also in the direct path of the Skinwalker, at least according to the Ute tribes that lived adjacent to the property. The Skinwalker is considered to be a shape-shifting entity with tremendous power, capable of wielding its power in unique and vast ways.

After the Gorman family (later identified as Terry and Gwen Sherman[73]) purchased the 480-acre ranch in 1994, they quickly discovered why it was avoided. The gamut of high strangeness ran rampant—from UFOs, to ghosts, aliens, Bigfoot, crop circles, animal mutilations, psychic phenomena, strange creatures, shadow beings, glowing orbs, poltergeist-like activity—you name it, it had it.

---

72 Corso, Philip J. with William J. Birnes. *The Day After Roswell.* Pocket Books/Simon & Schuster, 1998.

73 Lineup, The. "Skinwalker Ranch: Utah's Hotbed of Paranormal Activity." *The Portalist.* Open Road Media. 28 Sept. 2016. Web. 21 May 2018. https://theportalist.com/skinwalker-ranch-utahs-hotbed-of-paranormal-activity

In 1996, the National Institute of Discovery Sciences (NIDS), set up by Robert Bigelow, purchased the property to conduct an eight-year study of it, which was chronicled in the book, *Hunt for the Skinwalker: Science Confronts the Unexplained at a Remote Ranch in Utah* by Colm A. Kelleher, Ph.D. and George Knapp. Those involved thought that whatever was responsible liked to play games with them whenever they attempted to document and understand it, almost as if the phenomenon made an effort to display its power, but only on its terms and for a brief period of time.

Knapp alluded to further implications of the phenomena in an interview with Corbell. He explained that in some of the experiences, the consequences went well beyond the limits of the property. In his observation, it wasn't simply a haunted ranch in that the activity stayed confined to that particular area, but rather it moved and traveled. Knapp said that not only did the original ranch owners have things follow them after they left, but other investigators who had seen things there also had it follow them too.[74]

With reports of witnesses to UFO occupants, sightings don't always stop with just one encounter. The occupants might routinely revisit the same people over the course of a lifetime, or quite frequently within a brief period of time. In the 1950s and 60s, these people were hailed as contactees, whether they voluntarily signed up for the role or not. Some may think that these people are simply magnets for activity, but I think it might be that an individual has just become ultra-aware of the phenomena, and thus also more welcome of its presence, whether they consciously make that choice to welcome it in or not.

With Katie, the medium I mentioned earlier, her ability to audibly hear ethereal entities quickly became an annoyance. There were times when it was difficult for her to focus on her schoolwork while spirits of the deceased approached her in class wanting to have a chat. This would often happen to her whether or not she was ready for it. The spirits would just barge into her life, and at the time she had no idea how to keep them out.

Perhaps the same principle can be applied to the UFO phenomenon. Once the door to that reality is acknowledged, there might not be a way to close it again. Apply this concept on a grander scale. Let's say an influential leader made a public address to reveal that alien beings do exist. People might not panic, but the consequence in accepting that reality could

74 Corbell, Jeremy. "Hunt the Skinwalker." *Vimeo.* 27 Apr. 2017. https://vimeo.com/214982290

permanently remove the thin veil that separates our world and theirs. In turn, the phenomenon now becomes part of our reality simply upon acknowledgement and inadvertent invitation. Sure, it's making contact; just not the contact humanity had hoped for, especially if the beings aren't here to save the planet, but rather manipulate it.

It would seem that the subjects of ghosts and sixth senses are easier to talk about for most since it's a topic they can better relate to. Compared to its extraterrestrial sibling or its hairy cryptid cousin, there's a greater chance someone you know has either had a psychic experience or encountered ghostly phenomena. You might have experienced it yourself. As worldwide as the UFO phenomenon happens to be, it's still quite rare to witness these otherworldly objects, let alone the beings that are associated with it. Personally, I've never seen a UFO, either.

When it comes to the study of ufology, the experiences themselves can differ greatly from one encounter to the next. Because of this, UFOs are tougher to logically digest, even for the seasoned researcher. The paranormal world commonly defies expectation at every turn while the UFO experience seems to steer around the curves of the supernatural highway much more so.

I will listen to all accounts in an attempt to identify similarities and commonalities within both the paranormal cases and UFO reports. Let's focus more on the overall patterns that are displayed instead of trying to label the experiences under this category or that category. We will no doubt stumble upon something at some point that will shatter our previous notions on what the phenomena was capable of, anyway. The importance of remaining objective and considering all possibilities, following the data where it leads, is key. Like the existence of God, which scholars and scientists often try to comprehend within a two-dimensional frame of reference, the supernatural is clearly multi-dimensional, which we should be approaching outside of conventional modes of thinking.

Disinterest Built on Fear

John Keel did not consider himself a paranormal investigator, nor a ufologist, but rather a *Fortean.* This is a person who looks into all aspects of high strangeness, and not just one particular side of it. When I'm looking to connect with other researchers and investigators, especially those whose sole focus is on the paranormal, one of my first questions is, "What is your interest in UFOs?" More often than not, the answer is met with a mild to lack of interest, or even worse—fear.

As strange as it seems that our bold ghost hunter friends (who deal with malevolent forces capable of tossing about large objects or leaving physical scratches in people) are more fearful of three- and four-foot entities with barely enough strength in their stick bodies to support their oversized heads, there is probably another reason for it. Alien beings are much harder to prove and there's a guaranteed risk of ridicule associated with it. The topic deals with a force that has no apparent agenda, no clear motive, and a shape-shifting presence more difficult to track than a double agent in a James Bond novel.

Mysterious happenings also tend to surround those who get involved. Like I mentioned earlier with the psychic backlash concept, noted researchers like Keel have also pointed this out as well. In Keel's book, *Operation Trojan Horse* he chronicled many of the things which occurred to him in 1966-67 after he had begun his full-time effort into investigating UFOs.

Some of the effects which took place for Keel included bizarre telephone messages left from "space people," black Cadillacs that would mysteriously disappear on dead-end roads, luminous aerial objects that would follow him, and huge dark apparitions standing over him. He reported checking into a motel once, completely chosen on a whim, only to discover that someone else had made a reservation in his name. When he arrived, there were even a series of nonsensical phone messages waiting for him! Some of Keel's closest friends, who had no interest in the subject whatsoever, would experience poltergeist-like phenomenon taking place in their own homes.[75] (To those of my friends reading about this for the first time, please forgive me if that happens to you too.)

Although extraordinary, these disturbing aspects are certainly not unfamiliar to the seasoned investigator of high strangeness. Yet for plenty of others, the reason to avoid UFO research is rooted within the notion that human beings generally fear what they do not understand. With the ghostly realm, paranormal investigators have tricked themselves into believing that they might have more of that figured out than any so-called alien agenda. It's even scarier to consider that almost a hundred years after

75 Keel, John A. "Breakthrough!" *Operation Trojan Horse.* IllumiNet Press, 1996. pg. 243.

the birth of modern ufology, we aren't even close to cracking the question of who the visitors or observers are and why they are here.

The only thing we do seem to know is that something is taking place involving millions of people all over the globe, and has been since the very beginnings of human history.

Perceptions in the UFO Experience

The classic disc-shaped flying saucer is ingrained in the minds of most when they think of UFOs. But that visual representation is hardly the only form they take. In the 1990s through early 2000s, there was an explosion of reports that detailed triangle-shaped and deltoid craft in the skies above the US and the UK. These shapes were consistent in their appearance and movement—completely black but often brightly lit, flying at low altitudes and at low air speed, and usually totally silent. Widespread speculation surfaced that these sightings were merely covert testing of military aircraft.

The NIDS team conducted an analysis of the sightings during that time, from three reporting databases—their own, MUFON, and researcher Larry Hatch—and discovered the sightings to be contrary to previous covert flights of stealth aircraft, such as the F-117 and B2. Those aircraft were flown at night and over sparsely populated areas. But sightings of these "black triangles" as they came to be known, often took place near heavily populated areas, or along interstate highways at low altitude in plain sight of witnesses.[76]

Surprisingly, these shapes are much less reported than other shapes and only account for about ten percent of the case reports into MUFON. Yet out of that ten percent, the triangle sightings generally make the top 30-50% of the more interesting cases overall, because they are so impressive.[77]

If we examine what was widely reported back in the early days of ufology, it would appear that the objects are changing or evolving over time. Instead of flying saucers we are now seeing flying triangles. Instead of physical, metallic discs glistening in the sky, there are now countless

---

76 David, Leonard. "Silent Running: 'Black Triangle' Sightings on the Rise." *Space.com.* Purch, 02 Sept. 2004. Web. 06 Nov. 2017. https://www.space.com/302-silent-running-black-triangle-sightings-rise.html

77 "Robert Powell, MUFON Top 10 UFO Cases of 2015." *Open Minds UFO Radio.* Open Minds Production/Blog Talk Radio, 17 Oct. 2016.

reports of self-illuminated spheres and balls of light, which make up the vast majority of sightings. Either the occupants of these craft are changing up their design patterns or we are merely changing our perceptions of them.

Researcher MJ Banias brings up a great point in that we don't exactly know where the physical connection lies between the UFO seen as a physical object or thing, and the person that sees it.[78] Is the witness truly seeing a physical machine, or is the human brain simply interpreting the UFO to look like something we can better identify—be it a saucer, a triangle, or a glowing sphere?

He further argues that there might rather be a "paranormal half-way point" where humanity extrapolates information on to the UFO object, to make it look like something, whereas the UFO is actually something more mystical that doesn't have a defined shape in our reality. Perhaps UFO sightings are more of a mystical anomaly that use human cultural constructs to shape itself so that we can physically see and identify with it.[79]

This is certainly not a foreign concept to mankind. In the Christian Bible it is referred to as a *theophany*. For example, whenever God appeared to chosen individuals, He appeared in various forms they could physically observe—such as burning bushes,[80] pillars of clouds or fire,[81] or a storm.[82] God would also frequently take on the shape of an angel[83] or several angels,[84] before later taking on the human form of Jesus. And look at how Jesus spoke to His disciples too—opting for parables instead of direct answers to questions, which served to illustrate theological principles they could better grasp.

John Keel uncovered numerous examples, which seemed to suggest that the phenomenon is also imitative. For example, in January 1973, a witness in Ohio sketched in great detail an unusual looking helicopter

78 "MJ Banias, Philosophy in Ufology." *Open Minds UFO Radio.* Open Minds Production/Blog Talk Radio, 16 Jan. 2017.

79 "MJ Banias, Philosophy in Ufology." *Open Minds UFO Radio.* Open Minds Production/Blog Talk Radio, 16 Jan. 2017.

80 *The Bible.* Exodus 3:2, New International Version, Biblica, 1973, 1978, 1984, 2011.

81 *The Bible.* Exodus 13:21, New International Version, Biblica, 1973, 1978, 1984, 2011.

82 *The Bible.* Job 38:1, New International Version, Biblica, 1973, 1978, 1984, 2011.

83 *The Bible.* Judges 6:11, New International Version, Biblica, 1973, 1978, 1984, 2011.

84 *The Bible.* Genesis 18:1-2, New International Version, Biblica, 1973, 1978, 1984, 2011.

which she had observed. The UFO investigator who she showed it to (who also happened to be an aeronautical engineer specializing in helicopters) was quite astonished since what was drawn was a secret helicopter still in the conceptual stage.[85]

Noted international psychic Ingo Swann brought up a related perspective that he observed while pioneering the art of remote viewing. He and his team at Stanford Research Institute (SRI) learned that when remote viewers perceived something they didn't understand, they tend to explain it in ways that made sense to them. He referred to this as *analytical overlay,* or the ability of the mind to overlay something unknown, unrecognized, or unfamiliar with a mental image that is recognized.[86]

Apparently, people do this all the time whenever they encounter something they do not understand. According to Ingo, they usually arrive at an interpretation that really doesn't have much to do with what was actually experienced, either. He called this a *reality hopper,* which is just a clever way to describe how a person forms a vehicle of conclusion that may not, and probably does not, pertain to the actual reality of what was initially experienced. In other words, people fill in the unknown with what fits their known.[87]

The drawback here is in our limited interpretation of the supernatural experience as a whole, or rather the perceived experience. The more the witness is asked what they sensed, the more likely it is that they will rely on analytical overlays to better assess and comprehend the experience.[88] Ingo put it best by stating that we explain what we do not understand through whatever we think we do understand.[89]

One such case from the Paramus, New Jersey area accurately illustrates this. A gentleman reported a pine tree that floated along and kept pace with his car on the Garden State Parkway in 2002. He saw that it was the same color and shape of the natural trees around him—and even composed of

---

85 Keel, John A. *The Mothman Prophecies.* 1975. New York: Tor Books, 2002. Pg. 102-103.

86 Swann, Ingo. "Seeing One." *Penetration: The Question of Extraterrestrial and Human Telepathy.* Kindle ed., Panta Rei/Crossroad Press, 2014. Location 1221-1229.

87 Swann, Ingo. "Seeing One." *Penetration: The Question of Extraterrestrial and Human Telepathy.* Kindle ed., Panta Rei/Crossroad Press, 2014. Location 1229-1236.

88 Swann, Ingo. "Seeing One." *Penetration: The Question of Extraterrestrial and Human Telepathy.* Kindle ed., Panta Rei/Crossroad Press, 2014. Location 1244.

89 Swann, Ingo. "Seeing One." *Penetration: The Question of Extraterrestrial and Human Telepathy.* Kindle ed., Panta Rei/Crossroad Press, 2014. Location 1252.

pine needles—before it shape-shifted into a "swirling, bubbling mercury," shot up into the sky and disappeared.[90]

What if people began seeing giant ice cream cones floating in the sky instead? I imagine that this type of visual is so preposterous that witnesses would be inclined to stay silent or deny ever encountering such a thing. How many of these "floating ice cream cone" scenarios exist today, which go unreported simply because they don't fit into the classic experience we have come to associate with UFOs?

We should be asking ourselves if we haven't become somewhat accustomed to associating sleek, silent, speeding spaceships based on what we *think* these entities should be driving. We should also be questioning whether the drivers of said craft are actually beings from other planets as well. Why? Just look at how their origins have changed throughout recent years.

Prior to the modern age of ufology (the late 1940s), the alien entities might have been referred to as witches or demons. In the 1950s and 1960s, people said they came from Mars. Then it changed to Venus. Then the reports became a little more sophisticated in the 1970s—did they come from the Alpha Centauri or Zeta Reticuli star systems? In the 1990s, it evolved into another galaxy, then another dimension. Today, people view them as possibly being from another time or reality altogether. Could the visitors simply be an ever-evolving reflection of what we currently subscribe to?

Then there are the phantom helicopters that are seen either in pursuit of or within the vicinity of the UFOs. These helicopters can seemingly just show up (sometimes out of nowhere) and disappear just as suddenly too. How they are connected to the UFOs is a great mystery as they are also frequently reported with the cattle mutilation and crop circle cases. I've started to take note that they even show up over the houses of abductees or individuals who have had some bizarre experiences in general. Are the helicopters ours, or is it something that might also be part of the UFO experience?

It's easy to jump to the conclusion these must be the work of monitoring military or government organizations, as most, but not all, appear to be black with no identifiable markings on them. Yet this doesn't

---

90 Moulton Howe, Linda. "Alien Camouflage in 3-D Holograms and Screen Memories." *Earthfiles.* Earthfiles.com, 30 Jun. 2017. Web. 01 Jul. 2017. https://www.earthfiles.com/news.php?ID=2541&category=Environment

explain away the other characteristics, which some of these phantom helicopters exhibit—like flying in complete silence or shape shifting into other objects.

One example is a case that took place over three nights in late October of 1975 at Loring Air Force Base in Maine. Objects were reported that looked like helicopters and acted like helicopters yet didn't behave in a manner similar to helicopters—nor did they make any sound. The case was investigated by a total of twelve agencies,[91] including the United States Air Force, the FBI, NORAD, and the National Guard, trying to figure out why these objects were flying over the base, which had also been storing nuclear weapons.

On the first night at 7:45 pm, Staff Sgt. Danny K. Lewis was on duty when he spotted what he thought was an aircraft flying at low altitude along the northern perimeter of Loring. Lewis watched as the unknown aircraft penetrated the perimeter at an altitude of approximately 300 feet. From his location, Lewis could see a red navigation light and a white strobe light on the craft.[92]

The initial description is consistent with a helicopter's navigation lights. According to the National Investigations Committee on Aerial Phenomena (NICAP), the craft came to within 300 yards of the weapons storage area at an altitude of 150 feet and circled the base for about an hour, and then disappeared from radar, which indicated the object had landed or dropped below radar coverage. Security was increased at the base that first night as they presumed it was a helicopter because of its flight characteristics and size.[93]

On the second night at about the same time, sergeants at the base reported more lights from what they thought belonged to another helicopter. This time the lights were described as a white flashing light and an amber or orange light. The craft appeared and disappeared from

---

91 Open Minds Production. "The Truth about UFOs and Military Secrecy – Open Minds Magazine" Online video clip. *YouTube.* 28 Oct. 2016. https://youtu.be/k3d3KJbD1zw

92 Fawcett, Larry and Barry Greenwood. "Subject: Intrusions at Loring AFB - 1975." *NICAP.* Nicap.org/Francis L. Ridge, 30 May 2007. http://www.nicap.org/articles/CI-Loring.htm

93 Fawcett, Larry and Barry Greenwood. "Subject: Intrusions at Loring AFB - 1975." *NICAP.* Nicap.org/Francis L. Ridge, 30 May 2007. http://www.nicap.org/articles/CI-Loring.htm

view, then subsequently shut off its lights and reappeared over the weapons storage area at about 150 feet.[94]

Nick Redfern, who has extensively looked into this mystery, claims that he has more than twenty reports in his files alone. These reports outline black helicopters flying silently, which morphed into either the shapes of classic 1950s-era flying saucers, small balls of light, or large, blinding balls of light.[95]

Nothing is as it Seems

Appearances can be deceptive within the spectrum as a whole, but there's another angle to contend with too—trusting authority figures at the heart of the UFO matter. It's evident in numerous reports of official-looking authorities quick to the scene following a UFO event. It's even something that the U.S. government was well aware of and looked into first-hand. In early 1967, a memo written by Hewitt T. Wheless, Lt. Gen. USAF and Assistant Vice Chief of Staff, went out to all commands within the Pentagon...

> *"Information, not verifiable, has reached headquarters USAF that persons claiming to represent the Air Force or other Defense establishments have contacted citizens who have sighted unidentified flying objects. In one reported case, an individual in civilian clothes, who represented himself as a member of NORAD, demanded and received photos belonging to a private citizen. In another, a person in an Air Force uniform approached local police and other citizens who had sighted a UFO, assembled them in a school room and told them that they did not see what they thought they saw and that they should not talk to anyone about the sighting. All military and civilian personnel and particularly information officers and UFO investigating officers*

94 Fawcett, Larry and Barry Greenwood. "Subject: Intrusions at Loring AFB - 1975." *NICAP.* Nicap.org/Francis L. Ridge, 30 May 2007. http://www.nicap.org/articles/CI-Loring.htm

95 Redfern, Nick. "Black Helicopters: What In Hell?!" *Mysterious Universe.* Mysterious Universe/8th Kind Pty. 02 Nov. 2016. http://mysteriousuniverse.org/2016/11/black-helicopters-what-in-hell

who hear of such reports should immediately notify their local OSI (Office of Special Investigations) offices."[96]

The Pentagon spokesman for Project Bluebook*, Colonel George P. Freeman, had looked into a number of cases where civilians where threatened after their UFO sighting. His research indicated that "these men are not connected with the Air Force in any way."[97] Col. Freeman also went on to say that whoever these impersonators were, in posing as Air Force or government officials, they also committed a federal offense. Yet the perpetrators were never caught it seems and continue on to this very day.

*The official USAF study into UFOs in the 1960s.

Given this possibility in the UFO phenomenon, we cannot assume that if individuals present themselves as military or various alphabet letter agency representatives, that this is who they really are. As much as it seems like a ridiculous *X-Files*-esque scenario to even contemplate, it's not just a conspiracy theorist's dream. We know that the FBI looked into reports of the Men in Black in the 1950s according to various memos. J. Edgar Hoover, the FBI director at that time, wondered who the impersonators were that claimed to be from his office and why they were intimidating UFO witnesses.[98]

John Keel chronicled lots of these occurrences and I have no doubt they are still occurring today, even though the golden age of ufology has long since passed. As Keel was also quick to point out, we should not assume anything when it comes to the origin of these impersonators, either. He noted at the time that even though most of the manifestations which accompanied the UFO phenomenon didn't seem to fit into the

96 Wheless, Hewitt T. "Impersonations of Air Force Officers." USAF Memo. U.S. Department of the Air Force. 01 Mar. 1967. (Also included in: Keel, John A. *The Mothman Prophecies.* 1975. New York: Tor Books, 2002. pg. 25.)

97 Steiger, Brad and Sherry Hansen Steiger. "Aliens and the Space Program." *Ufos Are Here! Unmasking the Greatest Conspiracy of Our Time.* Citadel Press / Kensington Publishing Corp., 2001. pg. 122.

98 Redfern, Nick and Andy Roberts. "Saucer Secrets: The Real Men in Black." *Strange Secrets: Real Government Files on the Unknown.* Paraview Pocket Books, 2003. pg. 135.

conventional beliefs held by the saucer enthusiasts, details of such events were instead carefully ignored, and even suppressed.[99]

But trusting those who merely *appear* official isn't just a supernatural matter. It can be especially daunting when it comes to trusting all the anonymous sources that plague UFO research too. Anonymity in this field can quickly become just as deceptive as the nature of the phenomena itself.

The efforts of Richard C. Doty for example, show how seemingly trusted inside sources can also be rather unreliable. Doty was a special agent with the Air Force Office of Special Investigation (AFOSI) in the 1980s and was partly responsible for spreading the disinformation and misinformation within the UFO community.[100] It is well-documented how he and his associates quickly moved among the shadows using various monikers and false identities to disseminate information within the field.*

*One tactic used quite often to discredit UFO investigators and witnesses alike is to make them appear foolish or crazy so they are destroyed by their peers, or ultimately destroy themselves. Tragic examples like the Paul Bennewitz affair is a textbook case of how this works. Bennewitz was an electrical physicist who was led to believe that aliens had invaded Kirtland Air Force Base in New Mexico, among other things. But when he approached officials at Kirtland with his findings, he was fed false information by the likes of Richard Doty and others within the AFOSI, to perpetuate this belief in alien conspiracies. Some argue that that belief eventually drove Bennewitz to have a mental breakdown. Doty has argued that this was necessary to protect the more real programs Bennewitz actually uncovered. (For more information on this case check out Greg Bishop's book, *Project Beta: The Story of Paul Bennewitz, National Security, and the Creation of a Modern UFO Myth*, published by Paraview Pocket Books in 2005. Or check out the 2013 documentary, *Mirage Men* based on Mark Pilkington's book, *Mirage Men: An Adventure into Paranoia, Espionage, Psychological Warfare, and UFOs*, published by Skyhorse Publishing in 2010.)

Revelations of active disinformation may not come as any real surprise, but it may anger those who have spent their whole lives looking for truth behind the UFO mystery only to find an empty hall of smoke and mirrors at the end of it. We must question everything in light of these admissions, including those events that have become staples of UFO lore. But we don't need guys in suits spreading lies to get us to believe anything nowadays.

---

99 Keel, John A. *The Mothman Prophecies.* 1975. New York: Tor Books, 2002. pp. 9-10.

100 Rojas, Alejandro. "Ex-Air Force Law Enforcement Agent Says He Hoaxed Major UFO Mythologies." *HuffPost.* Oath/HuffPost/HPMG News, 13 Jul. 2014. Web. 06 Nov. 2017. https://www.huffingtonpost.com/alejandro-rojas/exair-force-law-enforceme_b_5312650.html

The "I want to believe" mantra is fast spreading within the likes of online forums and social media, replacing what was once a slow-moving, orally passed on tradition of the human experience. Websites such as YouTube and Reddit are probably some of the biggest perpetrators we face in today's inadvertent fake news with regard to the strange. It's great to see so many people interested in the topic, but nothing is fact-checked beyond that. Tales are just shared and reposted from one digital campfire to the next in our age of information, as well as fabrication.

Yet the UFO community continues to hold credence in the anonymous government whistleblowers that have information to provide, but refuse to disclose their true identities. Even if it's a trusted source to some, it's a source that cannot be followed up with in regard to their credibility or motives if the rest of us never know who that source really is. This makes it impossible to determine if it's legitimate material to consider or if we're just being taken for another ride on the eventual misinformation merry-go-round. Oftentimes these same shadowy sources like to play the card of having exclusive knowledge they want to disclose to the public, so they manipulate the researcher to believe that they have been handpicked to be the hero in disseminating it in order to help the disclosure process. How surprised some might be if they learned that a number of their own trusted sources were actually one and the same as the anonymous sources of the next researcher feeding them the same bogus material!

For this reason, I'm hesitant to give any credibility to the reports from insider sources who choose to keep themselves cloaked in anonymity. The UFO phenomenon is confusing enough to deal with all of the various angles and apparent disinformation schemes. But it is more challenging, and certainly more heartbreaking, when we have to question the very people we thought we could trust from the beginning. I've been down this road a number of times myself and I'm sure you have too.

The true trickster at play not only dwells in the shadows of the supernatural, but also in the hearts of men.

I want to believe.

"The real truth is that the UFO cultists have been played for suckers for years, not by the government, but by the phenomenon."[101]

– John Keel

101 Keel, John A. "You Can't Tell the Players Without a Scorecard." *Operation Trojan Horse.* IllumiNet Press, 1996. pg. 262.

Peculiar Visits

It's hard to consider the possibility that some of these entities take on human forms in an attempt to "fit in," yet there's more than enough testimony that could suggest this. As unsettling as the notion may be, we have to carefully consider the encounters with non-human entities (NHE) as not just UFO- or paranormal-related, nor even cryptid-connected, but all of the above and more.

Shape-shifting beings have been part of folklore and modern mythology in one aspect or another, so it should come as no surprise when we see it creep up in the modern reports too. Whether or not society chooses to accept the UFO phenomenon, peculiar visits from peculiar *people* just seem to be another aspect to the spectrum.

Experiences of this sort are often unable to be neatly categorized within one section or subsection of Fortean research. The NHE don't appear to be ghosts or aliens per se, yet they possess various similarities of each. They may be entities that come from the same place, or completely different places altogether. They could be spiritual beings, demons, robots or androids for all we know.

Whatever they are, they certainly leave a physical impression on our world and yet operate from within the invisible realm outside of it. Their presence is a conundrum of reality and non-reality congregating at the street corner of madness—the zip code of the spectrum.

Confusion and Intrigue Bathed in Black

There are far less people who are familiar with the Men in Black (MIB) reports than I thought. Some of that is brought on by a popular misconception within the UFO field that MIB are seldom encountered today as much as they were in their heyday—the 1950s and 1960s. Encounters with the MIB (and not just *men* in black, but also women) are quite unsettling, given that it appears their agenda is focused on intimidation, fear, or just general creepiness. Almost all of the encounters tend to center around UFO witnesses, UFO investigators, or those that are connected to the first two groups by unlucky association.

Other mentions of Men in Black conjure up images of the 1997 film by the same name, starring Will Smith and Tommy Lee Jones. Although that film is entirely a work of fiction, the basis of the subject matter is rooted deep within both paranormal and UFO lore. Reports of similar beings in black have been around much longer than we think, just in different contexts, like those found within the Middle Ages, Celtic lore, and even ancient Asian traditions.

The stereotypical MIB, as we've come to identify nowadays, truly took hold after Albert Bender's intriguing encounters from 1953, later chronicled in his book *Flying Saucers and the Three Men*. Other accounts like Bender's quickly followed at that time. The MIB's preferred choice of black attire and black vehicles often characterized them, as they began to show up at homes or at workplaces, or wherever the targeted individual was, often times alone. These curious fellows usually asked the individual questions about their own experience, which later evolved into acts of deterrence, threats, or intimidation. Then as quickly as the MIB had arrived, they'd disappear without a trace. These encounters were quite effective in keeping certain people, like Bender, from further discussing their experiences.

Two of Bender's closest friends, Dominick Luchesi and August C. Roberts, observed that he had become a changed man after the visit by the three men. Bender dropped all of his UFO research and assumed another identity managing a hotel somewhere in California to escape the MIB's lingering effects. They noted that Bender later suffered from severe migraines, which Bender believed were caused by "them" whenever he talked about the topic.[102] Maybe Bender's fears got the best of him, and the lingering physical effects he suffered from were psychosomatic. Yet there are other reports that suggest the MIB have the ability to affect people on a physical level too.

For example, there was the case of bogus Air Force officer "Major Smedley" in 1968 that investigators Brad and Sherry Steiger specifically looked into.[103] This Major Smedley spoke with a peculiar accent and did not drive any sort of automobile whatsoever when he showed up to interrogate a civilian UFO researcher in Jamestown, NY. Maj. Smedley left that investigator with an acute headache and temporary amnesia, as he could recall nothing about their conversation for about five minutes afterwards. Later, this same Maj. Smedley resurfaced in Pennsylvania (again without a vehicle) to interrogate a second UFO researcher about a case he was working on, leaving him violently ill and confined to a bed for two weeks.

In numerous instances, the MIB identify themselves as working for some non-existent branch of government, or even a fake civilian organization. It was from these phony credentials that people speculated the MIB to have been military or government—or even the aliens themselves—minimizing the flow of UFO information or spreading disinformation around to muddy it. The overall purpose of the MIB still remains hazy but after examining the reports, it seems that their agenda centers around information extraction, as well as information suppression.

---

102 Steiger, Brad and Sherry Hansen Steiger. "Aliens and the Space Program." *Ufos Are Here! Unmasking the Greatest Conspiracy of Our Time.* Citadel Press / Kensington Publishing Corp., 2001. pg. 123.

103 Steiger, Brad and Sherry Hansen Steiger. "Aliens and the Space Program." *Ufos Are Here! Unmasking the Greatest Conspiracy of Our Time.* Citadel Press / Kensington Publishing Corp., 2001. pg. 124.

At the 1967 Congress of Scientific UFOlogists conference in New York City, John Keel revealed that the MIB sometimes silenced UFO witnesses before the witnesses even had time to report their sightings![104]

There is also reason to believe the MIB could take on other identities depending on the circumstance. Some reports indicate they've posed as poll takers or salesmen, for example, instead of the authority figures or government officials we've become accustomed to hearing about.[105] Instead of trying to collect data or sell something to the targeted individual, these MIB appear more interested in asking personal questions of them, or of the incident they witnessed—a telltale marker of the MIB M.O.

Keel was able to document several of these reports, including instances of them masquerading as census takers. The census takers would inquire into things such as the witness' interest in flying saucer sightings, or whether or not the individual thought the Air Force was withholding information on the topic.[106] Odd questions to be asked on a supposedly official census form!

Sometimes the MIB even pose as social workers and offer to take pictures of UFO witnesses' entire families. The phantom social workers (PSW) or bogus social workers (BSW) that were largely reported in the 1980s and 1990s mirrored the motif of the MIB reports. As researcher Emma McNeill explains in *Fortean Times...*

> *The basics of an encounter today remain the same as in the Nineties heyday of the BSW. An unrecognised person calls on a family and says that he or she is from an official child welfare service and claims to be looking for signs of abuse or neglect. The caller is normally a woman, sometimes working with a "colleague". She may have an odd appearance, such as wearing a wig or unusual clothing. There is an examination of the child or children and in some cases an attempt to take the child away. After the visit, the parent realises they have been duped and*

104 Steiger, Brad and Sherry Hansen Steiger. "Aliens and the Space Program." *Ufos Are Here! Unmasking the Greatest Conspiracy of Our Time.* Citadel Press / Kensington Publishing Corp., 2001. pg. 123.

105 Beckley, Timothy Green. "Introduction: Watch Out Behind You! By John A. Keel." *Mystery of the Men in Black: The UFO Silencers.* Inner Light Publications, 1990. Pg. 5

106 Skinner, Doug. "Special Cases – The Long Island File (20): The Census Taker." *John Keel: Not an Authority on Anything.* WordPress, 26 Dec. 2016.. Web. 27 Jun. 2017. http://www.johnkeel.com/?p=3067

that the authorities have no record of the caller. After an initial isolated case there may be a wave of similar reports. A couple of weeks later, cases dry up.[107]

Dan Aykroyd, well-known for his work in Hollywood's greatest comedic films like *Ghostbusters* and *The Blues Brothers,* is also well-versed in the subject. It's an interest that has been long-held throughout his family, actually. This interest led him to begin production on a TV series for the Syfy channel in 2002 titled, *Out There.* The series centered on UFOs in particular as he interviewed some highly credible people to speak on the subject—like Colin Andrews (crop circles), Linda Moulton Howe (cattle mutilations) and John Mack (alien abductions).[108]

During a break in filming the final episode with UFO disclosure activists, Dr. Steven Greer and Stephen Bassett, something odd happened to Aykroyd. As he went outside for a cigarette break between the interviews, Britney Spears called him. It was in regard to an episode of Saturday Night Live that she had wanted to do with him. While he was in the midst of the call, he happened to glance across the busy New York City intersection at 42nd Street and 8th Avenue and saw a black Ford sedan. He noticed that the license plate looked "fuzzy" but it was "definitely a police car." He described, "two guys were there, and a big, big tall guy got out of the back seat." The tall guy stood in the street and looked directly at Aykroyd with a "real dirty look." Aykroyd turned to look the opposite direction, then immediately back over again, and the three men and car had vanished. Two hours later, he was informed that the series had been canceled without any further explanation.[109]

What Aykroyd recalls is classic in MIB reports, however, in a large number of cases, MIB won't be seen arriving in any vehicle, and will just suddenly appear, almost out of thin air. They also arrive solo, in pairs or groups of threes. Their demeanor is typically reported as robotic, mechanical, and devoid of any emotion. If they do elicit emotion, it appears overtly intentional or forced, just as their physical appearance seems slightly off

107 McNeill, Emma. "Return of the Bogus Social Workers." *Fortean Times.* Dennis Publishing, n.d. Web. 27 Jun. 2017. http://subscribe.forteantimes.com/blog/return-of-the-bogus-social-workers

108 *Dan Aykroyd Unplugged on UFOs.* Directed by David Sereda, Graviton Entertainment, 15 Jul. 2005.

109 *Dan Aykroyd Unplugged on UFOs.* Directed by David Sereda, Graviton Entertainment, 15 Jul. 2005.

as they try to blend in with the surroundings, yet fail miserably in an attempt to seem more human than they are. MIB try to enunciate proper English, but generally listen more than they speak, as they have a tendency to blunder names and details on occasion. In the instances where there is more than just one, it is typically only "the leader" that speaks, while the others just observe.

When the MIB are present, it doesn't seem to be for an extended amount of time, almost as if they are running off some sort of energy source that directly affects their motor skills and communicative ability. It appears this seems to deteriorate rapidly the longer they are present. But their movements are very mechanical, clunky, or just noticeably awkward right from the beginning.

Contrary to the popular notion that the MIB are strictly black suit and black hat-clad beings, they have also been reported in brown suits, striped ties, and even fedoras with white bands.[110] Facial characteristics of the MIB can vary too but seem to follow a common appearance. Most describe them as either deathly pale, with deep suntans or very olive in complexion. They could have hair that seems phony, or no facial hair, head hair or sideburns whatsoever. Their eyebrows may even appear painted on and their lips an obvious red, like lipstick.

Such was the case with family physician Dr. Herbert Hopkins on the evening of September 11, 1976 in Old Orchard Beach, Maine. Dr. Hopkins received a phone call around 8:00 pm from a man identifying himself as vice president of the New Jersey UFO Research Organization, an organization that never existed at that time.[111] The caller explained that he wanted to talk to Hopkins about his research into a case involving an abductee named David Stephens.

What is particularly troubling about this case is something Dr. Hopkins talked about in a 1978 radio interview. Dr. Hopkins mentioned that he always asked unknown callers to identify their credentials. Yet, on that particular occasion, he admitted that he never asked for the man's name, which perplexed him. Then mere seconds from when Dr. Hopkins

---

110 Redfern, Nick. "Do All M.I.B. Wear Black?" *Mysterious Universe.* 8th Kind Pty Ltd, 05 May 2018.. Web. 10 May 2018. http://mysteriousuniverse.org/2018/05/do-all-m-i-b-wear-black

111 Speigel, Lee. "'Men In Black' Inspired By Scary Stories Of People Who've Seen UFOs." *HuffPost.* Oath/HuffPost/HPMG News, 23 May. 2012. Web. 06 Nov. 2017. https://www.huffingtonpost.com/2012/05/23/men-in-black-inspired-ufos-government-agents_n_1536996.html

hung up the phone, the man had already made his way up the steps to his door—a seemingly impossible feat given that the nearest phone booth was across the street. And again, Dr. Hopkins admitted that it was uncharacteristic of him to be so relaxed and open to willingly let a strange man into his house too.[112]

The man was dressed in a brand new, pristine black suit with a dark blue shirt as he entered Dr. Hopkins' home. When he removed his black derby hat, Dr. Hopkins saw that he was as bald as an egg. He had smooth, plastic-like dead white skin, absent from a single piece of hair on his body along with no eyebrows, nor eyelashes. He noted that the man had an oddly placed small nose and small ears set far back on his head too. His mouth was just a straight slit with lips that were described as a brilliant, ruby red. Whenever he wiped his mouth with the suede gloves he wore, a bright red mark was left behind on them and the red on his lips smeared, almost like he had just applied lipstick to give the appearance of lips.[113]

The encounter culminated with a strange threat. The man made a penny dematerialize in the palm of Dr. Hopkins' hand as an example of what they could do should Dr. Hopkins decide to pursue the Stephens case or UFOs any further. Towards the end of the visit, the man's speech was quieter and slower as he staggered in his movement. He told Dr. Hopkins that his energy ran low and eventually left as quickly as he had entered. Shaken up so much by the event, Dr. Hopkins destroyed the rest of the files on the case that very same night.[114]

---

112 Hopkins, Herbert. Interview. 23 May 1978. *The Wendy Connors' Faded Disc Archive.* "High Strangeness: Men in Black, Mothman, Flatwoods Monster, Hairy Bi-Peds in UFOs, Allende & Philadelphia Experiment, Richard Shaver & Gray Barker (Disc 10)." Audio. https://archive.org/details/HighStrangenessGuide and http://www.project1947.com/shg/connors/audiodisc.html

113 Hopkins, Herbert. Interview. 23 May 1978. *The Wendy Connors' Faded Disc Archive.* "High Strangeness: Men in Black, Mothman, Flatwoods Monster, Hairy Bi-Peds in UFOs, Allende & Philadelphia Experiment, Richard Shaver & Gray Barker (Disc 10)." Audio. https://archive.org/details/HighStrangenessGuide and http://www.project1947.com/shg/connors/audiodisc.html

114 Hopkins, Herbert. Interview. 23 May 1978. *The Wendy Connors' Faded Disc Archive.* "High Strangeness: Men in Black, Mothman, Flatwoods Monster, Hairy Bi-Peds in UFOs, Allende & Philadelphia Experiment, Richard Shaver & Gray Barker (Disc 10)." Audio. https://archive.org/details/HighStrangenessGuide and http://www.project1947.com/shg/connors/audiodisc.html

Enter the Hairless Clones and Accompanied Weirdness

It would seem that these sorts of remarkable encounters with the MIB are rarely reported in our current age, but do not be mistaken—they still exist! The documentation to back up any type of MIB encounter is even rarer still, yet in one case, they were actually captured on videotape. Security camera footage circulated by the Aerial Phenomenon Investigations team (API)[115] apparently showed two MIB as they entered the front lobby of the Sheraton Fallsview Hotel in Niagara Falls, Ontario, Canada on May 10, 2009. According to witnesses who interacted with them first-hand, these MIB were in search of the hotel's manager—Shane Sovar.

Usually it's a quick turnaround for these "UFO silencers" to arrive on the scene, or at the doorstep of a witness following their sighting, but with the case of Shane, the MIB didn't make an appearance until about seven months later. On October 14 of the previous year, Shane and Burt[116] (the hotel's security manager) witnessed a black triangle-shaped UFO, which hovered silently over the property at about 10:30 pm.[117]

As the two men looked out onto the Niagara River that night they saw a light emanating downward from an aerial craft, which Shane said

115 "Actual MIB Footage." *Coast to Coast AM.* Premiere Radio Networks, (n.d.). Web. 08 Jul. 2017. http://www.coasttocoastam.com/videos/19798/45703/Actual-MIB-Footage/#!/19798/45703/Actual-MIB-Footage

116 Sovar, Shane. Telephone interview. 03 Mar. 2018.

117 "UFO sightings in the Falls." *Niagara This Week.* Metroland Media Group, 07 Nov. 2008. Web. 08 Jul. 2017. https://www.niagarathisweek.com/news-story/3281808-ufo-sightings-in-thefalls

they initially assumed was the Coast Guard at the time.[118] A lot of people mistakenly go into the river, so it wouldn't have been unusual to see helicopters that night fishing for bodies. But as soon as Shane suggested to Burt a second possibility—that it was either the Coast Guard, *"or a UFO"*—the light went from shining down on the water to shining up directly at them.

The craft then slowly shifted its trajectory towards them. Shane decided to get a better view as he made his way towards the hotel, but Burt remained where he was. As the craft floated over top of Shane, he realized it was a lot bigger—as large as a football field, to be exact. He could also see the shape of the craft in greater detail, which was described as triangular with three white lights, one on each tip along with a big, red light underneath that pulsed like a heartbeat. The craft made no sound whatsoever as it literally crawled over top of him—practically hovering. As it was directly overhead he had the thought that whatever he was looking at was "not from here."[119] But by the time it reached the field across the street, it took off in the blink of an eye and was gone.

As Shane shared his experience at work the next day, one of the hotel bellmen confirmed that several other black triangles had also been reported in the Fort Erie paper.[120] At the bottom of those reports there was the name of a UFO researcher who was specifically looking into the cases. That investigator was Brian Vike of HBCC UFO Research in British Columbia, who Shane later reported his sighting to.[121] Although lead API investigator Marsha Barnhart looked into the MIB aspect that later followed, API's published report also noted that there were numerous UFO sightings regarding the same type of triangular craft, which was seen along both the Canadian and U.S. sides of Niagara Falls in 2008.[122]

About a week later, the craft came back to visit the Sheraton Fallsview hotel. At approximately 2:30 am, one of the hotel guests notified Shane that he had a big pothole in the parking lot. As he grabbed a pylon and

---

118 Sovar, Shane. Telephone interview. 03 Mar. 2018.

119 Sovar, Shane. Telephone interview. 03 Mar. 2018.

120 Sovar, Shane. Telephone interview. 03 Mar. 2018.

121 "UFO Sighting Report – Canada / October 14th 2008: Niagara Falls, Ontario." *UFOINFO.* UFOINFO, 12 Nov. 2008. Web. 08 Jul. 2017. http://www.ufoinfo.com/sightings/canada/081014b.shtml

122 Paris, Antonio. *Aerial Phenomena: Reviving Ufology for the 21st Century.* Antonio Paris, 2012. Pg. 48.

made his way over to the far end of the lot, something just told him to look up.[123]

In the sky was the same type of triangular craft he had seen previously, but the second sighting was at a much higher altitude. Shane knew it was the same craft since it had the same shape and light formation, so he ran to the top of the parking garage to get a better look. The craft hovered directly over the hotel again, then zipped straight down into the Niagara River and disappeared. In sheer disbelief that this had happened a second time, he returned home and relayed the sighting to his wife. She had been highly skeptical of the first sighting, yet after hearing a similar account from her hairdresser earlier in the day, she was left with no reason to doubt her husband after all.[124]

Fast forward seven months later to the MIB encounter. Although Shane had taken the day off at the time of their visit, some of the other hotel staff were there, and described to him the next day their odd interactions. The two men were described as not only identical to one another in their height and stature (both extremely tall), but also in their faces (with extremely pale skin), their clothing (matching black suits and fedora hats), and the fact that they lacked any facial hair whatsoever (nor even eyebrows or eyelashes).[125]

It's unsettling enough to hear how the MIB can easily creep out a UFO witness, but those merely associated with or connected to a witness in some way can also be subjected to their disturbing demeanor. One of the hotel bellmen, a man named Ricardo,[126] was the first one to encounter the MIB as they entered the hotel lobby...

> *"They asked for (redacted), for the Manager. And I told them; 'well he's not here. Do you want to talk to someone else?' And they said, 'no we just want to talk to (redacted).' And that was the end of our conversation."*[127]

---

123 Sovar, Shane. Telephone interview. 03 Mar. 2018.

124 Sovar, Shane. Telephone interview. 03 Mar. 2018.

125 StewieBlackOps. "The real Men in Black caught on tape?" Online video clip. *YouTube*. YouTube, 19 Apr. 2012. Web. 08 July 2017. https://youtu.be/bcToNxPvZAE

126 Sovar, Shane. Telephone interview. 03 Mar. 2018.

127 Barnhart, Marsha. Email interview. 23 Dec. 2017. (Note: Marsha redacted all the names in her original report to protect the anonymity of those involved. She did not provide any additional names to me.)

Even though his initial conversation with them was short and uneventful, it was their startling appearance that made more of an impact...

> *"That was what, uh, really kept my attention. These guys were really tall, probably taller than average people. But what really caused me a bit of curiosity was they were just looking identical. They were just look-alike. While I was talking to them I was trying to look for any differences. I just couldn't believe it, but they were exactly identical. ...They looked human to me...except that they were identical. I didn't have too much time to talk with them. I just remember they weren't old. They didn't look young; they didn't look either too old or too young."*[128]

Regarding their skin tone and the hats they wore (later identified as Fedoras), the bellman stated...

> *"Uh, well it was pale. They had hats. And they were dressed all in black. It was a little bit shocking to see people dressed like that in that moment. But I didn't have much time to talk to them."*[129]

When the bellman revealed to the MIB that Shane wasn't at the hotel, they gave him a look like, "we don't believe you" and continued on to the next person in the lobby—a woman named Maria who was the hotel tour desk operator at the time.[130]

Maria also provided Shane with her testimony about the two MIB, but she had had a lengthier conversation with them—and one that affected her even more. She was almost in tears describing the ordeal as she revealed some of the things they discussed—things which made absolutely no sense to her, yet involved governments and conspiracies.[131] But again, it was the MIB's distinct characteristics and overall demeanor that had a more profound impact on her. The description was consistent with the bellman—no facial hair, eyebrows, or eyelashes—yet it also appeared that they wore wigs attached to their hats. Their eyes were unusually large and

---

128 Barnhart, Marsha. Email interview. 23 Dec. 2017.

129 Barnhart, Marsha. Email interview. 23 Dec. 2017.

130 Sovar, Shane. Telephone interview. 03 Mar. 2018.

131 Sovar, Shane. Telephone interview. 03 Mar. 2018.

distinctively blue; so much so that she felt hypnotized since the MIB never blinked and responded like they could already read her mind. So, she was trying not to think about Shane during her time with them. But somehow, the two men already *knew* what she was thinking, although she didn't know how that was even possible to begin with.[132]

One of the more puzzling questions Shane and I wrestled with in our conversations was that if these MIB seemed to know everything already, then why hadn't they just come in on a different day altogether, and one that Shane would've been working? If these individuals can read minds, it doesn't appear that they have very smart minds operating within themselves.

When he reached out to his parking attendants for clues as to where the men could've possibly originated, the mystery expands out further. The attendants could see that the men had parked along the far island of an adjacent hotel, but they couldn't determine the exact make or model of the vehicle they had arrived in. They could only identify that it was an all-black car with completely black windows, which prevented them from seeing any further inside it. The vehicle also didn't have any license plates on it, either.

The only reason the security camera footage of the two MIB entering the lobby exists is because of the foresight from the hotel's director of security—who also happened to be Burt's brother. Shane hadn't discussed the MIB visit with the security director when a copy of the footage suddenly showed up on his desk. He said, "Look Shane, I don't know what happened to you and I don't know who these guys are, but I want you to keep this, just in case anything happens to you. This whole scenario and situation is freaking the hell out of me."[133]

Shane then handed that footage off to Marsha and the API team, and eventually it made its way online where anyone can view it for themselves. Certainly, people complain that it's not the greatest quality of video, which is always to be expected since no piece of paranormal footage is ever good enough, and even the best footage is too good, altogether. Plus, for whatever reason, the owner of the hotel didn't want to invest in a newer security system. The case was frequently made to upgrade, even before this incident, but the request was rejected since the existing system was adequate enough, at least in the eyes of the hotel owner. Now had the

132 Sovar, Shane. Telephone interview. 03 Mar. 2018.

133 Sovar, Shane. Telephone interview. 03 Mar. 2018.

system been upgraded, Shane says that that footage of the two MIB who entered the hotel lobby that day could have been as clear as a bell.[134]

But regardless of whether or not the MIB were filmed at all, were these guys even *human* to begin with? According to the bellman's account…

> *"Uh…they, they sounded human to me. I can't say they didn't sound different than human. Other than… they were just, I would say, what I said to (redacted), was they were clones. They were just, one exactly same to the other. They were identical.*[135]

This description of MIB or NHE appearing identical, or even clone-like, is something that creeps up time and again in numerous cases of high strangeness which follow the initial UFO event. Another good example can be found with Michael and Ryan—two individuals who came forward in 2014 after hearing about Shane's case on Marsha's *API Case Files* podcast.

In 2001, Michael and Ryan decided to stop off at a local mini mart that ran parallel to Interstate 8 near San Diego, California. As they pulled in, Michael noticed a military convoy was also parked nearby, which piqued his interest since he had grown up on a military base. Though he wasn't aware of any active military units in that particular area, he found himself compelled to survey the scene. While Ryan stayed at the pump to fuel up their vehicle, Michael went inside to purchase some food and drinks. Inside the store, Michael observed a total of nine soldiers, all the exact same size and the exact same height, lined up in tight single file at the counter, ready to pay for their exact same items. He noted that there were no military insignia or identification on their uniforms. All of the soldiers had their covers (or caps) on. This was another observation that didn't make any sense to him since virtually every soldier will remove their cover indoors, unless they are under arms. Plus, their caps were pulled so low over their faces that he couldn't even make out their eyes. As Michael got in line behind them to make his purchase, he began to stare at the back of one of the soldier's heads and found there was not a single piece of hair, nor a single pore on his skin. The skin tone also looked unnatural and

134 Sovar, Shane. Telephone interview. 03 Mar. 2018.

135 Barnhart, Marsha. Email interview. 23 Dec. 2017.

rubbery, like one of his daughter's Barbie dolls, as Michael best described it.[136]

The look-alike soldiers all followed the same action and gestures in each paying for their single item—which happened to be just one gallon of water. Michael remembers the cashier repeating the sale total ($1.09) to each soldier individually, who would then pull out two dollars from the same side pocket, place it on the counter, collect the change, then turn and walk out the door in the precise identical manner. None of the soldiers even uttered a word to the cashier. This course of action repeated for each and every one of them. When Michael got another chance to look at their faces as he headed out of the store, he saw that they all shared the exact, identical facial features too, and not a single difference in any one of them! After he returned back to his vehicle, Michael asked Ryan to go back into the store for himself in order to verify what he had seen. Ryan returned less than twenty seconds later, just as creeped out as Michael had been.

The two men waited for the soldiers to leave the premises and then proceeded to follow them, out of curiosity. The convoy headed westbound on S80 (Evan Hewes Highway) towards San Diego, while Michael and Ryan paralleled them on I-8 (Kumeyaay Highway) for about four to five miles, before they literally saw them drive into the side of a mountain and disappear. Michael has had UFO experiences before, but as Marsha put it best, what are we to make of these high strangeness events that seem to ride the coattails of UFO experiencers?[137]

Believe it or not, the MIB aspect following Shane Sovar's two UFO sightings isn't the end to his story, nor is it the only incident of high strangeness which surrounds him. Soon after the UFO sightings is when things began to get equally as weird, in and around his home too. The initial occurrence took place about a week following his second sighting, when he was outside cleaning the leaves out of the gutter. Out of his periphery Shane noticed an older, noticeably short man who approached his property. The man wore a suit with a jacket on top, as well as a hat. He stopped in front of the house and just smiled.

As Shane came down off his ladder the man stated, "I built this house."

---

136 Aerial Phenomena Investigations. "Episode 3 - High Strangeness in the California Desert." *API Case Files.* 21 Mar. 2014. Web. 06 Jan. 2018. http://apicasefiles.libsyn.com/episode-3

137 Aerial Phenomena Investigations. "Episode 3 - High Strangeness in the California Desert." *API Case Files.* 21 Mar. 2014. Web. 06 Jan. 2018. http://apicasefiles.libsyn.com/episode-3

"Oh, you're the original owner?" Shane asked.

"Yes, I built this house," the man confirmed, quite happy with its appearance and beaming with joy. He asked to see the backyard, where the first thing the man noticed was the sunroom, which pleased him greatly. Shane informed him that he had not built it, but that the owners prior to him had.

"My gosh, the trees are so big now! They're so big!" the man went on as he was led to a larger area that sloped down. "My daughters used to roll down those hills."

"That's nice," Shane responded.

"Okay, I'm going to go now," the man said as he shuffled down the sidewalk, taking small steps that appeared as if his feet weren't even lifting off of the ground. As he departed, he mentioned to Shane, "I'll see you next year." The statement didn't seem particularly strange at the time, but could it have been a precursor to the MIB encounter the following year?

A few weeks later Shane was out talking with his neighbor Nancy and mentioned his random meeting with the old man who had claimed to be the original constructor of the house. Nancy, who had lived next door for some 60+ years, was dumbfounded once she heard his description of the man.

"You gotta be kidding me," she said, "He's dead. That man died like fifteen years ago!"

We also have the peculiar aspect of subtle manipulation in terms of the way the experiencer interacts with and responds to the experience itself. Thinking back on the manner in which Shane conducted himself while interacting with his ghostly guest, he never once made contact with the man, nor even extended a handshake to greet him or say goodbye. Given Shane's profession of meeting new people on a daily basis, he admits this would have been an unusual reaction *not* to do.[138]

From that point on, more paranormal activity would take place—from toys operating on their own in the middle of the night (even with the batteries taken out of them), to phantom footsteps and strange clicks and beeps on his landline telephone. Items would also abruptly go missing only to reappear somewhere else, along with intense feelings of being observed by some unseen presence. The activity would die down for a while but then ramp back up days later. It was a very scary time to be in the house. So

138 Sovar, Shane. Telephone interview. 03 Mar. 2018.

much so, that he and his wife had even considered selling the property just to escape it.

It was prescribed by one of his colleagues to burn sage—everyone's favorite metaphysical cure-all—in an attempt to rid the house of any negative energy. Which of course, Shane did try, most like everyone who goes through these ordeals, but it had no noticeable effect, most like everyone who goes through these ordeals, apart from the realization of feeling foolish in the process. As random as the activity first began, it also ended randomly too, yet diminishing significantly after the MIB encounter.

Bizarre events still tend to occur occasionally from time to time, yet thankfully not to the level or frequency that they had been occurring at that time.

But why him? Shane can't tie the two incidents together (the UFO sightings and the MIB event). He feels that instead it may have been that a door was opened somehow during his sightings, and perhaps that was why the activity took place afterwards.[139]

Yet if it were only that easy, then it wouldn't be referred to as the UFO *enigma*. Solid investigators like Marsha Barnhart know just what to look for—patterns in the phenomenon, as well as in the experiencers of the phenomenon itself. At one point, she asked him to think back throughout his childhood and take note of anything else that would have set itself apart as being out of the ordinary.[140] And sure enough, when he reflected on it, there were in fact a couple of incidents that stood out as somewhat strange.

One event Shane remembers was in the seventh grade, which would have been sometime in the early 1980s. He and a friend both decided to take a shortcut through the forest in order to visit a new corner store that had opened up, shortly before Shane had to be back home in time for dinner. He remembers the sun was setting when his friend noticed a glowing orb coming at them through the trees. The sight was terrifying for whatever reason, so they took off running. But the only thing beyond that that Shane remembers is opening up the front door to his house and his mother asking where the hell he had been. Confused at that time, he replied that they had just gone to the corner store, or so he thought. However, he never remembers physically going to the corner store—only running from the glowing orb and then arriving home. There was also

139 Sovar, Shane. Telephone interview. 03 Mar. 2018.

140 Sovar, Shane. Telephone interview. 03 Mar. 2018.

nothing to suggest a definitive time delay either, apart from his mother telling him that his family had had dinner an hour ago, without him.

A second incident he recalls was when he was eighteen and his family just moved into a new house. He woke up in the middle of the night, sensing a presence and seeing small people in his bedroom. But he was unable to move or scream. All he could do was move his eyes. Could it have been a bout of sleep paralysis or something more? Whatever it was, he recalls being absolutely terrified, but cannot recall much of what happened beyond that.

Has any of his kids had any strange experiences? Well, there is something that stands out as particularly intriguing. His son, who was five or six at the time, drew a picture with little beings with big eyes around his bed. When Shane inquired as to who they were, his son responded…

"Oh, they're the little ones that visit me."[141]

Character Flaws

We may not be able to answer every question we have in regard to the spectrum, but we can continue to look for patterns that lead us in some sort of direction. One of the patterns we should make note of is this element of confusion which seems to surround it. Not only are the various experiences within the spectrum perplexing, but there's also the air of credibility we have to contend with in the experiencers themselves. Some factors go without question in establishing a person's level of credibility, but should we dismiss someone's experience altogether because of say, one particular character flaw or undesirable personality trait?

For example, in the Dr. Herbert Hopkins case I mentioned earlier, Herbert's late nephew Howard called into question his uncle's account altogether in an online blog published in 2008. The site has since been taken down, but in it Howard referred to his uncle as a genius, but also someone who was a "fantasy-prone individual, craved the center of attention and limelight and on a base level he sometimes just made things

141 Sovar, Shane. Telephone interview. 03 Mar. 2018.

up—no matter how hyperbolic—to top everybody else."[142] He further characterized his uncle as alcoholic and delusional, "tripping over the 'invisible dog'" repeatedly in the middle of the night and blaming it for such things, even though the real dog remained on the bed next to Howard the entire time.[143]

Nevertheless, Howard presents some insight into additional strange events which trailed the Hopkins family long after Herbert's initial MIB encounter. Herbert's son John (Howard's cousin) and his wife Maureen experienced another aspect to the puzzling MIB/NHE nature, which was far less sinister but equally as disturbing.

On September 24, 1976—two weeks after Herbert's initial MIB encounter—Maureen received a strange phone call from a man that claimed he knew John and wanted to visit the couple. John went to the local restaurant to pick up both the man and the man's female companion. Even though they were strangers, John still felt compelled to invite them back to his home anyway, which was eerily similar to his father's experience. The strangers' appearance and posture were described as peculiar as they wore odd, old-fashioned clothes and took short steps while simultaneously leaning forward as they walked, almost as if they were afraid to fall.[144]

John noted an abnormality with the way the woman's legs were joined at the hips, along with having breasts that were set unusually low. Once he arrived back at the house, the strange couple asked both him and Maureen a series of rather mundane questions—things like what they watch on TV, or what they read in books, or what the two of them talk about most of the time.[145] On the surface, that might have been simply small talk in how people often inquire about the weather or the traffic, even though it's not that important to us. Yet, in the case of these two strangers, it just marked the beginning of their odd behavior.

---

142 Hopkins, Howard. "The Truth About a Man in Black." *Dark Bits.* Blogger, 13 Jan. 2008. Web. 06 Jul. 2017. https://web.archive.org/web/20080524015603/http://howardhopkins.blogspot.com/2008/01/truth-about-man-in-black.html

143 Hopkins, Howard. "The Truth About a Man in Black." *Dark Bits.* Blogger, 13 Jan. 2008. Web. 06 Jul. 2017. https://web.archive.org/web/20080524015603/http://howardhopkins.blogspot.com/2008/01/truth-about-man-in-black.html

144 Hopkins, Howard. "More MIB Weirdery." *Dark Bits.* Blogger, 23 Jan. 2008. Web. 06 Jul. 2017. https://web.archive.org/web/20080723185406/http://howardhopkins.blogspot.com/2008/01/more-mib-weirdery.html

145 Hopkins, Howard. "More MIB Weirdery." *Dark Bits.* Blogger, 23 Jan. 2008. Web. 06 Jul. 2017. https://web.archive.org/web/20080723185406/http://howardhopkins.blogspot.com/2008/01/more-mib-weirdery.html

During the meeting, the man fondled his female companion and asked John and Maureen if he was "doing it right." When John later excused himself, the man asked Maureen "how she was made" and whether she had any nude pictures of herself. After an uncomfortable set of further exchanges, the strangers quickly excused themselves and left the home without even a goodbye.[146]

That side of the Hopkins family abruptly moved from Maine to Florida shortly thereafter and without much notice; perhaps to escape all the weirdness? Howard dismissed most of that weirdness altogether based on his opinion of his uncle, as well as his recollection of John and Maureen's alternative lifestyle choices.[147]

There are no doubt questionable aspects to almost every unusual story today's investigator will hear, but I challenge us to examine all of the evidence—and not just bits and pieces. Deception, disinformation, and confusion have surrounded the phenomena at its core. It rarely ever appears to be a simple black and white issue in these types of remarkable cases. There are plenty of gray areas too, which keeps it both interesting and incredibly frustrating. (I wonder if the alien grays chose their grayish skin as a sort of visual metaphor...)

If individual witnesses demonstrate consistent deceptive practices or disillusion, this might suggest some sort of mental issue at its root. And if that is the case, then of course all testimony should be called into question and/or disregarded. But it would be foolish of us to toss out the baby with the bathwater in other cases simply because there might be one or two questionable aspects that are indirectly related to the experience. Of course, each and every aspect should be considered in how it ties in to the testimony, but we should also be examining the motives behind the witnesses and considering whether or not the deception comes from a conscious intent to deceive, or rather if the deception emanates directly from the phenomenon itself.

Some time ago, friends of mine became involved with a demonology case, in which the individual at the center of the activity was caught hoaxing some of the evidence presented to the investigators. It reminded

146 Hopkins, Howard. "More MIB Weirdery." *Dark Bits.* Blogger, 23 Jan. 2008. Web. 06 Jul. 2017. https://web.archive.org/web/20080723185406/http://howardhopkins.blogspot.com/2008/01/more-mib-weirdery.html

147 Hopkins, Howard. "More MIB Weirdery." *Dark Bits.* Blogger, 23 Jan. 2008. Web. 06 Jul. 2017. https://web.archive.org/web/20080723185406/http://howardhopkins.blogspot.com/2008/01/more-mib-weirdery.html

me of the Enfield poltergeist case from 1977. Even though that case is widely considered to be one of the most well-documented and observed cases of paranormal activity, eleven-year-old Janet Hodgson and her elder sister Margaret were caught numerous times as they played tricks on the investigators, confirmed by both Guy Lyon Playfair[148] and Maurice Grosse.[149]

But there were events that occurred in the Enfield case that the girls couldn't have hoaxed. Such things as levitation, furniture being moved through the air, flying and apported objects, disembodied voices, and even teleportation, which were all amazingly documented and observed by numerous witnesses at various times. Carolyn Heeps, a policewoman who was called out to the scene at the time, signed a sworn affidavit that she saw a large armchair move unassisted four feet across the floor.[150]

This spectrum of strange phenomena seems to enjoy its covert nature, so it should come as no surprise when we encounter many different angles that require us to question the legitimacy of the experiences and the witnesses themselves.

Strangers and Stalkers and Smiling Men

Timothy Green Beckley and James Moseley are two notable figures in ufology that have taken a lot of flak, but they have no doubt made significant contributions also. It was these two men that took a photo in 1968 in Jersey City, NJ of another purported MIB. It was taken at the height of the 1965-68 UFO flap that had occurred up and down the east

---

148 Penman, Danny. "Suburban poltergeist: A 30-year silence is broken." *DailyMail.com.* Associated Newspapers/The Daily Mail. 05 Mar. 2007. Web. 08 Aug. 2017. http://www.dailymail.co.uk/news/article-440048/Suburban-poltergeist-A-30-year-silence-broken.html

149 Storr, Will. "The Conjuring 2: what really happened during the Enfield Haunting?" *The Telegraph.* Telegraph Media Group. 13 Apr. 2017. Web. 08 Aug. 2017. http://www.telegraph.co.uk/films/2016/06/13/the-conjuring-2-what-really-happened-during-the-enfield-haunting

150 Brennan, Zoe. "What IS the truth about the Enfield Poltergeist? Amazing story of 11-year-old London girl who 'levitated' above her bed." *DailyMail.com.* Associated Newspapers/The Daily Mail. 04 May 2015. Web. 08 Aug. 2017. http://www.dailymail.co.uk/news/article-2054842/Enfield-Poltergeist-The-amazing-story-11-year-old-North-London-girl-levitated-bed.html

coast, with a cluster of cases that involved apparent non-human entities in the New Jersey and New York regions.

John "Jack" Robertson was an investigator that had amassed a large body of data in regard to not just UFOs, but also cryptids reports. He claimed that whenever he went to work in the daytime, his wife Mary saw a man dressed in black that watched their building from across the street. This man was observed on several occasions for four days straight.[151] He was described as "very, very wooden looking with a very pale face, kind of standing recessed back in a doorway across the street and dressed all in black with a black hat and a black suit on."[152] The couple had also received bizarre phone calls and hang-ups, and had case files directly related to the UFO phenomenon snatched from their house.

Beckley and Moseley decided to pay the Robertsons a visit to see if there was anything to the situation. Sure enough, as they drove past their building to look for a place to park, they spotted the strange individual as he had been described: black overcoat, black shoes, black pants and black hat. Beckley and Moseley snapped two photographs: one where he stood in a doorway as he peered off into the distance, and a second of his black vehicle. When the duo circled the block again, the man was gone and never seen again.

John Keel wrote about the same UFO flap, which included a series of events in and around the New Jersey Turnpike area. One of those reports occurred on the night of October 11, 1966 where two police officers reported a blazing white light in the area of Wanaque, NJ. On the same night, forty miles south in Elizabeth, two boys encountered a giant man over six feet tall dressed in a sparkling green coverall outfit that reflected the streetlights. The man suddenly appeared on the other side of a towering fence that separated the street from the turnpike and just grinned at them. How the man arrived on the other side of the fence, they couldn't figure out since it was impossible for any man to scale such a height. They described him as having a dark complexion, no hair, and "little

151 Redfern, Nick. "Photographic Evidence." *The Real Men in Black.* New Page Books/ The Career Press, 2011, pg. 63.

152 Beckley, Timothy Green, et al. *Curse of the Men in Black: Return of the UFO Terrorists.* Global Communications, 2010. pg. 91.

round eyes...real beady...set far apart."[153] They did not recall any ears, nose, or even hands.

Although bizarre, there's not much significance of a bright light and a weird grinning man seen on the same night, until you take into consideration that Moseley was also investigating that case with Keel, and it was Moseley who was with Beckley when he snapped the photo of the MIB later on in Jersey City. Could the MIB have been connected in some way? And if so, then how?

The grinning man seemed to pop up time and again in Keel's research. One such case involved a sewing machine salesman named Woodrow Derenberger, who upon driving home one night on November 2, 1966, noticed a bright object that dropped out of the sky and landed directly in front of his truck on the highway outside of Point Pleasant, WV. A six-foot tall man with a dark complexion and slightly elongated eyes approached him. The man also wore a dark coat and blue trousers, which were described as "quite shiny and had a glistening effect."[154] This man grinned fixedly at Derenberger and communicated telepathically, identifying himself as a being named "Cold." Derenberger soon developed regular occurrences with this "Cold" character and referred to him as "Indrid Cold."

A few days after Derenberger's sighting, the first reports in West Virginia surfaced of the infamous Mothman—a winged humanoid creature that had red, glowing eyes. During that time, there were also encounters with the MIB, and other peculiar NHE, reported concurrently with the Mothman sightings. Yet, it was not the only thing going on at that time. There were numerous UFO reports and other high strangeness.

Phantom Photographers

The strange becomes even stranger when these bizarre individuals creep around. Not only because of their odd appearance, but also because of their actions.

---

153 Keel, John A. *The Complete Guide to Mysterious Beings.* Rev. ed. New York: Main Street Books, Doubleday, 1994. Rpt. of Strange Creatures from Time and Space. Fawcett Publications, 1970. pp. 196-198.

154 Keel, John A. *The Complete Guide to Mysterious Beings.* Rev. ed. New York: Main Street Books, Doubleday, 1994. Rpt. of Strange Creatures from Time and Space. Fawcett Publications, 1970. 198-199.

In the 1960s, there were anomalous events taking place with so-called *phantom photographers.* Some of the reports echoed the MIB encounters, where the curious individuals would happen to show up out of nowhere to photograph UFO witnesses and even researchers, and then quickly vanish out of sight. In some cases, phone interference and general harassment would follow suit, leading those to suspect they were being stalked by government agents attempting to deter them from investigating the phenomenon.

Nick Redfern mentioned the phantom photographers in his research into both the Men in Black and the Women in Black (WIB). In fact, it was during his writing of both books on the topic that his publisher, Beth Wareham, had her own set of encounters with these bizarre beings.[155]

It was while Beth edited Redfern's book, *Men In Black: Personal Stories and Eerie Adventures,* that she became absolutely inundated with harassment from these MIB—everything from crackling phones to creepy voices coming on the line, to seeing these guys in the street. The experiences lasted for the entire duration of preparing Redfern's book, but they reached a fever pitch, she says, when the legs of a black figure darted past her in the bathroom mirror one evening.[156] The activity ceased shortly after that particular incident. It wasn't until she began work on Redfern's follow-up manuscript for *Women In Black: The Creepy Companions of the Mysterious MIB* that the activity ramped up again. A WIB had even waited for her on the stoop across the street from where she lived in New York City, just to let her know it was there. Thankfully it was the only WIB she encountered.

One specific incident stood out for Beth as particularly unnerving during the initial MIB infestation, but it didn't involve them, per se. Instead it centered on one of these possible phantom photographers. As soon as she stepped out the door to her brownstone, she encountered a man taking pictures of the front of it. He didn't look out of place but possessed some sort of large setup camera. It wasn't one of those old-fashioned cameras with a giant flash bulb, but still a rather large rig that stood out, especially in our digital era of slim and small pocket devices. In all her time living in that particular building, she had never seen anyone so fascinated with taking pictures of it like this man had been. Beth yelled at

155 Redfern, Nick. "The Strange Saga of the 'Phantom Photographers.'" *Mysterious Universe.* 8th Kind Pty Ltd, 10 Oct. 2016. Web. 26 Jun. 2017. http://mysteriousuniverse.org/2016/10/the-strange-saga-of-the-phantom-photographers

156 Wareham, Beth. Email interview. 27 June 2017.

him without hesitation and the man took off down the street, in a "goofy jerky-jerky with his legs," as she put it.[157] This was consistent with the other descriptions in the individuals she saw, who also seemed to have trouble controlling their bodies.

In Beth's view, they're not so much scary as they are just plain *goofy*. Though they annoyed her greatly at the time, she admits that it was quite comical too.[158] The MIB and WIB did not feel very threatening, though they made her question the reality of their existence on numerous occasions. The black-clad beings always appeared extremely thin, and whenever she'd yell at them, they jumped and suddenly disappeared. At first, she thought the experiences were all in her head since she was also working on a book about the topic. But then she'd experience them with another sense, like sound, for example, which was more often how she noticed them at first. But are these strangers real in the sense that they exist in our physical reality? Beth still isn't completely sure of that. Most of what she noticed visually was caught in her periphery—then *poof*—they would simply disappear, or turn around a corner and vanish. Since her reaction in the moment was characterized by a high level of stress, it is worth wondering if her state of mind was somehow "feeding" these beings with the ability to manifest? I've heard the same concept applied to negative entities on the paranormal front. Perhaps there is a direct connection between our emotional and mental states and glimpses into this other realm.

Some of the phantom photographers have expressed a keen interest in children, especially newborns of a UFO witnesses' family. They would offer to photograph these children, free of charge, but of course, the photographers didn't visit other new parents in the area. Family photographs and albums would also vanish from these same witnesses' homes, as Keel also noted in his findings.[159]

Geraldine Robinson, along with her late husband and two daughters, all had an encounter involving a phantom photographer on the Atlantic City, NJ boardwalk in July of 1974. A man suddenly "came out of nowhere" and started taking photographs of twelve-year-old Lisa and four-year-old Tina. The man seemed to be more focused on photographing Tina when

157 Wareham, Beth. Email interview. 27 June 2017.

158 Wareham, Beth. Email interview. 27 June 2017.

159 Skinner, Doug. "Organized Harassment of Individuals (7)." *John Keel: Not an Authority on Anything*. WordPress, 05 Mar. 2014.. Web. 27 Jun. 2017. http://www.johnkeel.com/?p=2205

Geraldine quickly took note of him.[160] Being a naturally protective mother, she instantly confronted him, and then in an instant, the man simply vanished. "I turned that quick—I turned to the kids, and I turned around—he's gone! Where the hell he went?" Geraldine described.[161]

Since we should always be looking for patterns in the phenomena, these beings could be even more timid than we realize. Confrontation or outright pursuit scares them off, as Timothy Green Beckley noted the same thing with the MIB, despite their untold capabilities to menace and strike fear into people. When we reverse the tables on them, they are motivated to make a quick exit.[162] Hot on the trail of the imitators, John Keel couldn't catch them, either. Whenever he'd receive a call that they were in the vicinity he would race over to catch them but would miss them by mere minutes.[163]

But what stood out vividly in both Geraldine and Lisa's recollection of their phantom photographer was his attire. He was covered completely in all dark clothes (either black or navy blue in color) with long pants, a long sleeve shirt and a blazer. "The way he dressed, I really remembered that. Nobody's on the boardwalk in the middle of July like that. I thought that was so strange," Geraldine added, considering that everybody else wore either shorts or a halter-top that hot summer day.[164] In Lisa's recollection, she didn't note anything else about his appearance other than he was Caucasian with long dark hair and taller than their father who was 5'9". Lisa also noted that he "wasn't a bad looking man and well built"[165] contrary to the pale, thin characteristics often characterized with these strange individuals.[166]

Such is the case with Dawn DeVito, who has had more than her fair share of run-ins with strange individuals, as I'm sure all women can relate.

---

160 Anhalt, Lisa. Phone interview. 16 May 2017.

161 Robinson, Geraldine. Phone interview. 16 May 2017.

162 Beckley, Timothy Green, et al. *Curse of the Men in Black: Return of the UFO Terrorists.* Global Communications, 2010. pg. 197.

163 Sheila Martin. "John Keel – The Men in Black (1989 Lecture) UFOs" Online video clip. *YouTube.* YouTube, 10 Dec. 2012. Web. 01 July 2017. https://youtu.be/mvm77diHCdA

164 Robinson, Geraldine. Phone interview. 16 May 2017.

165 Robinson, Geraldine. Phone interview. 16 May 2017.

166 Anhalt, Lisa. Phone interview. 16 May 2017.

One bizarre encounter stands out as particularly odd, which took place when she was only sixteen.

In 1986, Dawn and her friend Jenny were on their way to visit Jenny's father in Cedar Falls, Iowa where he worked as a local lawyer. When they parked the car, they noticed a very thin, short African-American man that had seemingly just appeared. "It wasn't until we parked, that he was just *there,*" Dawn explained. The man greeted the two girls with an "eerie, blank, half-smile" on his face. By the appearance of his ill-fitted clothes and demeanor, they just assumed he was homeless and tried not to pay much attention to him.[167]

But the man called out to the girls and asked them if he could look at their hands and read their palms. Contrary to Dawn's better judgment, Jenny was more than happy to do so as a naïve teenager. The man inspected Jenny's hands first without much reaction. But as he examined Dawn's he immediately turned pale, screamed in horror and ran away. Not quite sure what to do next, the girls instinctively ran after the man to find out what had driven him away so suddenly. The man ran with a limp, almost like one leg was shorter than the other, according to Dawn's account, but before they knew it, he had quickly turned the corner and disappeared. Dawn explained that where they were on the street, there were no other alleyways or other places the man could've physically ducked into to hide from them. He literally just vanished. Dawn is still bothered by the event to this day: "What is it about me that scared this guy? What did he see in my hand?"[168]

Dawn has had multiple experiences that run the paranormal spectrum. Her experiences are even similar to an abductee in that she has reported missing time, encountered and even photographed the classic gray alien entities, and witnessed numerous UFOs. But that's not all. She has also had poltergeist activity, shadow people encounters, and possesses various psychic abilities (along with her family). The Robinson family has also reported many strange experiences, especially precognitive abilities that have continued throughout future generations too. Another aspect worth mentioning with the Robinsons is that their entire family encountered anomalous aerial phenomena months prior to the phantom photographer. Geraldine and her husband saw an anomalous "exploding" object in the sky just a few months before. And a month after their sighting, their daughter Lisa, along with two of her friends, saw a saucer-shaped object

167 DeVito, Dawn. Personal interview. 11 May 2017.

168 DeVito, Dawn. Personal interview. 11 May 2017.

with flashing lights as it hovered above the row homes in their Northeast Philadelphia neighborhood.

The Beastie Boys and Mr. Seven-Fifty

Sometime during the late 1980s through early 1990s, eight to ten friends in the New York area came together to form a group called the *Arcadians.*[169] They were united by the paranormal in one way or another, either as the result of a personal experience or a natural curiosity of the topic, in general. For those that possessed more intuitive abilities, the group became a way to explore, investigate and better understand those abilities. For others still, it helped identify traits they may not have even realized they had to begin with.

I had the privilege to get to know some of the Arcadians over time, including Alan and Michael Lewis, two brothers who described in great detail the after-effects that the phenomena can exhibit, which also seem to echo various traits of the Men in Black experience too.

Some of the group members would become privy to certain psychical cues that would tip them off. For example, Alan might receive an extrasensory "alert" when one of these strange non-human entities were present.[170] While Michael, the youngest member of the group, developed a burning sensation in his ears, which was an indicator that a paranormal event had occurred or would soon take place. Christopher Di Cesare, another member of the Arcadians, likened it to a sort of "spiritual puberty" which Michael found himself in as he began to perceive the supernatural realms.[171] Chris had already been well-aware of such realms as a result of his own experiences (the widely known and well-documented C2D1 haunting), which took place during Chris' college enrollment at SUNY Geneseo in 1985.

As a result of the Arcadians' ongoing involvement with the paranormal, several of them discovered they were being watched, possibly even monitored at times. This surveillance often took the form of strange individuals they nicknamed the *Beastie Boys.* Although somewhat menacing in nature,

---

169 Lewis, Alan. Personal interview. 26 May 2018.

170 Lewis, Alan. Phone interview. 02 Jun. 2018.

171 Lewis, Michael. Personal interview. 24 Sept. 2016.

these Beastie Boys were not necessarily beastly looking, but rather was a reference to the hip-hop trio that was in the pop culture vernacular at that time. The Arcadians hoped that their code word would allow them to speak freely about their observers without making it apparent to the observers themselves. As much as the Beastie Boys attempted to appear human and fit in, it always came off as a failed attempt at best, similar in nature to how Men in Black also try to blend in. In some examples Michael gave me, the way they might move their bodies could pass as "normal," but their voices could be askew or vice versa. Or there could be something in their eyes that was slightly off—not as in a physical deformity, but moreover something which lacked consciousness, morality or principle. Things that make humans, well, human.

One of the more disturbing incidents which involved the Beastie Boys was after a series of vivid dreams and visions received by one of the group's more psychically gifted members. In his impression, he saw a UFO crash which happened just off of Long Island, near Lake Ronkonkoma, an area well known by the locals for its high strangeness. He felt a strong sense of urgency to visit the Lake Ronkonkoma County Park, as if something had reached out to him in distress there. The rest of the Arcadians agreed and arranged for an evening investigation as soon as possible.

When they arrived at the park, it looked to be in a stage of renovation, with concrete piping scattered throughout the area. Several of the more intuitive members received impressions that a being was trapped or possibly left behind, while other non-human entities were attempting to locate the being's whereabouts. It was a moment both exhilarating and frightening since no one could physically see them, yet just pick up on their energies. Although they sensed something wasn't quite right about the situation overall, it wasn't until they left the park that things took on the more visible Beastie Boys form instead.

On the return trip home, the group pulled in to a diner in Commack, NY and parked two spaces from another car with three men inside. The men looked eerily similar to one another and had the same height and build.[172] At first glance, they would have been easily missed, except that each one of them wore the same style of leather jacket, unlike any the Arcadians had ever seen before. They also talked very loudly, even though they were right next to each other, and held a distinctively gregarious laughter.[173] As the

172 Lewis, Alan. Phone interview. 02 Jun. 2018.

173 Lewis, Michael. Personal interview. 24 Sept. 2016.

Arcadians went inside, the men quickly followed and sat at a table directly across from theirs. Their loud conversation and distinct laughter continued to permeate throughout the diner, like they were trying too hard to "fit in."

At one point, Chris excused himself to the restroom in an attempt to clear his mind from the events earlier at the park. As he stood in solitude and began reciting a prayer of spiritual protection, one of the men entered the restroom, stood directly beside him, and proceeded to emit an unsettling and unearthly, high-pitched tone from his mouth. Chris quickly left the diner altogether after that and the rest of the Arcadians followed his cue. As they made their way out the door, the three men were already in their car, now parked two spaces on the opposite side of where it was before. How the men suddenly went from inside the diner to inside their car in the blink of an eye was astounding since no one had ever seen them actually leave the diner.

"Get better agents!" Alan shouted as they left the parking lot.

The Arcadians encountered a number of other disturbing Beastie Boys (and even Beastie Women) over the next several years, but their experiences transitioned into something else equally as puzzling. Nondescript sedans could be seen either following the group, crossing them at intersections, or parked and observing them from afar. They referred to these iterations as the *Mr. Seven-Fifties*—originating from the "MR750" New York license plate usually seen attached to them. Appearances usually took place whenever the group members got together or arranged to meet with one another. These vehicles might appear a couple times a week or even multiple times within the same day. The drivers of the Mr. Seven-Fifties weren't particularly social, unlike their counterparts who seemed to make more of an attempt to interact, for better or worse. But both forms always seemed to make a lackluster attempt to blend in while displaying their odd mannerisms.

During that time, Michael cleaned a series of medical offices off of Empire Blvd. in Webster, NY. They were located on the same side of the street as a local bank, not far from the Bay Town shopping center. As Alan and Chris waited for him to get off work one evening, they sat in the parking lot towards the rear of the bank. A dark blue Chevy Caprice pulled up just shy of the ATM. The driver—a slightly rugged six-foot-tall man dressed in a matching dark blue button-down with dark blue pants—exited the car and proceeded to measure the area around the ATM with a tape measure. The man went over the same area repeatedly without writing down any of his measurements. If it wasn't for the time of night this took place, especially next to a bank, they might have missed him. But Alan declared that as they watched the man it became clear that his actions made no rational sense to them. As they got the impression that they were somehow being observed and began to discuss this idea, the man quickly hopped back in his car and drove away.

Now we might consider this to be a case of just some poor contractor who could have forgotten an assignment from earlier in the day for a demanding employer, but the group noticed the same car following them later in the night. Not to mention, the MR750 plate attached to it was also seen by another Arcadian as it followed him earlier that same day in Henrietta. As Alan recalls, the plate designation stood out from the typical plate, so it was certainly something they couldn't mistake.[174] Perhaps it was a vanity plate. Yet when the Arcadians asked a law enforcement friend of theirs to run a check on it, they were astounded to learn that it had been a completely non-existent plate number!

Not all of the vehicles surveilling the group even carried a license plate to begin with. One of them, seen in Goshen, was a fairly sporty-looking model, unlike the rather lackluster sedans typically observed. This car was an odd dark green olor and appeared as if it was meant to attract attention. It had a strange bright glow surrounding the body and was quite unusual in its shape, Alan described.[175] He had never seen this type of car before, nor ever since, which was something like a cross between a Chevy and a Porsche. In the areas where there should have been a license plate, there was merely a neon green glow instead.

The green car passed them several times as the group was either outside congregating or driving on the road. At one point, Alan remarked that the windows on the car were tinted beyond the legal amount, effectively preventing them from seeing the driver.[176] The car seemed to respond to his comment, and on the next pass, the driver's side window was now completely open. Seated at the wheel, Alan observed a twenty-something man staring blankly ahead with extremely pale skin, blonde hair and an unusual haircut—one that was pushed back and standing up slightly, similar in style to something the singer Chris Issak might have

174 Lewis, Alan. Phone interview. 02 Jun. 2018.

175 Lewis, Alan. Phone interview. 02 Jun. 2018.

176 Lewis, Alan. Email correspondence. 27 Jun. 2018.

worn. The driver made no eye contact with them and just stared blankly ahead.

Even though the Arcadians' encounters don't seem to fit the mold with regard to the stereotypical MIB experience, they still share some notable characteristics in their appearance, mannerisms and observational tendencies. I wonder how many other reports of a similar nature exist that are simply disregarded because it's either too strange, or not strange enough. Perhaps we must be on the lookout for not only entities in black, but ones in blue, neon green, and whatever other color they decide to present themselves in. In the world we live in, we'd be naive to ever expect the world of the strange to adhere to any rules, let alone a single wardrobe.

Alan and Chris have also had particularly close encounters of UFOs together at the same time.[177] One was a saucer-shaped craft, which banked over their car at fifty to seventy-five feet away. This occurred while driving the New York State Thruway (I-90) through the Montezuma National Wildlife Refuge. A second was a completely stationary craft that hovered at one-hundred feet above them, as well as Chris' father, while on the Newburgh-Beacon Bridge, which crosses the Hudson River.

This region has long been associated with UFO activity for a number of years now, but one story stands out in particular when I think of the Arcadians.

John Ford was a MUFON researcher who investigated what he believed was a UFO crash that occurred on November 24, 1992 at Southaven Park in Shirley, NY.[178] This is about fifteen miles from Lake Ronkonkoma, the area where the Arcadians had originally picked up on their similar scenario. Was there a possibility that the two events overlapped? Or perhaps the Arcadians had a premonition of an event that was yet to come, since most of the activity centered around March of 1988 and January of 1991, according to Chris.[179] Maybe this explains some of the odd surveillance if the two events were somehow connected.

In a stranger plot twist, Ford was arrested four years later on June 12, 1996 and charged with attempting to poison three political officials by

---

177 Lewis, Alan. Phone interview. 02 Jun. 2018.

178 RebelSkum. "Wrongfully arrested UFO investigator, John Ford, still in mental hospital for over 20 years." *Steemit Beta / UFOs.* Steemit, 15 Feb. 2017. Web. 03 Oct. 2017. https://steemit.com/ufos/@rebelskum/wrongfully-arrested-ufo-investigator-john-ford-still-in-mental-hospital-for-21-years

179 Di Cesare, Chris. Correspondences via electronic messaging. 4 Oct. 2017.

sneaking radium into their cars and lacing their toothpaste with radioactive metal.[180] He was committed to the Mid-Hudson Forensic Psychiatric Center on an insanity plea,[181] but Ford, and several of his friends and colleagues, maintain his innocence and claim that the charges were merely a frame-up.[182]

It is a strange world we live in...

Impersonating the Impersonators

Not only do these forces imitate, but they also possess the ability to impersonate—including other investigators and researchers. Both John Keel and Brad Steiger experienced these doppelgangers on occasion, which both mystified and frustrated them, especially as they investigated witnesses that claimed they had already been there.[183]

Brothers Tim and John Frick are writers and paranormal investigators widely known for their work into the Mothman sightings. In their spare time, they also enjoy dressing up as the Men in Black, especially during the annual Mothman festival in Point Pleasant. The Frick brothers have also appeared as the MIB in several documentaries as well. So, it's safe to assume they are professional MIB imitators so to speak, even though the real MIB apparently don't take to it very kindly.

In early November of 2006, the Frick brothers visited their friend Shirley in northeastern Ohio. One week after their visit with Shirley, she sent them an email to ask if they had returned to her neighborhood

---

180 McQuiston, John T. "U.F.O. Fan Ruled Unfit for Trial in Long Island Murder Plot." *The New York Times*. The New York Times Company. 14 Nov. 1997. Web. 08 Jan. 2018. http://www.nytimes.com/1997/11/14/nyregion/ufo-fan-ruled-unfit-for-trial-in-long-island-murder-plot.html

181 RebelSkum. "Wrongfully arrested UFO investigator, John Ford, still in mental hospital for over 20 years." *Steemit Beta / UFOs*. Steemit, 15 Feb. 2017. Web. 03 Oct. 2017. https://steemit.com/ufos/@rebelskum/wrongfully-arrested-ufo-investigator-john-ford-still-in-mental-hospital-for-21-years

182 Colton, Michael. "Out There." *The Washington Post*. The Washington Post, 11 Jan. 1998. Web. 08 Jan. 2018. https://www.washingtonpost.com/archive/lifestyle/1998/01/11/out-there/89f520c3-bb7b-41d3-a991-6c4a1a2ff322

183 Keel, John A. "Men-in-Black Lore and the CIA." *Our Haunted Planet*. Second Edition. Fawcett Publications, 1971/Galde Press, 2002. pp. 98-99.

unannounced. They were confused because they hadn't returned, but apparently their MIB counterparts had decided to turn the tables and impersonate them for once.

According to the report,[184] Shirley had taken her dog out one night when she noticed a vehicle pull into the church parking lot across the street from where she lived. As two tall men got out of the vehicle they appeared to "walk funny." Shirley watched them with the notion it could have been Tim and John, only to have doubts when she realized the men were also watching her! Shirley went back inside her home but continued to monitor the situation through the safety of closed window blinds. A second vehicle also pulled in to the parking lot and a third man got out to talk to the other two. All three men then got back into their respective vehicles and drove off.

The next day Shirley tested out a baby monitor she planned to sell, and inadvertently picked up a stray phone conversation between her neighbors. Ironically enough, the neighbors talked about the strange men from the night before. Shirley learned that the third man had been one of the neighbor's sons and had gone out to confront the two tall men, since they regarded their presence suspicious at that time of night. The two tall men told the son that their names were Tim and John and that they were paranormal investigators! Even more peculiar was that in the week before, when the Frick brothers had visited Shirley, they talked with her in the same church parking lot at about the same time of night.[185]

Was this some sort of psychical "looped playback" of previous events, or a planned impersonation by active forces with an agenda?

After their meeting with Shirley that week, the Frick brothers drove on to another Ohio location where an unusual white van kept pace with them for over thirty minutes straight. It had passed them on the road several times, and through its slightly tinted windows, the Frick brothers could see three or four men inside wearing three-piece black suits—similar to their own MIB costumes, but without the black sunglasses. At one

184 Raynes, Brent. "An Interview with Timothy Frick: Writer, Cryptozoologist, and an MIB Impersonator (who the MIB may have impersonated!)" *Alternate Perceptions Magazine.* Issue #151. Alternate Perceptions Magazine, Aug. 2010. Web. 08 Aug. 2017. http://mysterious-america.com/frickinterview.html

185 Raynes, Brent. "An Interview with Timothy Frick: Writer, Cryptozoologist, and an MIB Impersonator (who the MIB may have impersonated!)" *Alternate Perceptions Magazine.* Issue #151. Alternate Perceptions Magazine, Aug. 2010. Web. 08 Aug. 2017. http://mysterious-america.com/frickinterview.html

point when the van was in front of them, they noticed the license plate read "111L" along with the words "Unregistered Vehicle" above it. Given the circumstances that would follow suit, they found the entire series of incidents more than a little eerie.[186]

Is Gary Sudbrink There?

The telephone is a popular instrument of high strangeness. From conversations with the dead, to correspondences with life forms from another time or place, to sudden interference in the midst of calls about this topic in general, there are a number of reports that seem to suggest something lurks in our telecommunication systems. Not only does it allow everyday creeps in their own perverted sense to use it to torment their victims, but arguably just as disturbing, it allows the other side to make contact with us as well. One such instance involved Gary Sudbrink, who I had initially been introduced to through MUFON Virginia state director Sue Swiatek, but then later reached out to and corresponded with on my own.

In 1993, Gary was an Air Force captain assigned to medical pharmacy work in San Antonio, Texas. On Sunday, February 7 of that same year, he planned an unannounced, surprise trip to visit family and friends in the Long Island area of New York, and that's where the strangeness really began to take off. At the airport where Gary waited to depart, he took note of two men that each initiated a conversation with him at different times. For whatever reason he cannot recall exactly what they conversed about, but he does remember pieces of it. Gary has a keen ability to recall his experiences with some of the most intricate detail, which is why I find the lack of conversational data somewhat odd in comparison to something insignificant, like his recollection of their hair color, for example.

Once the airline called out rows for Gary's flight, the first man with dark brown-hair approached him with a pen and pad and asked what his name was. Gary was hesitant to answer, and the man sensed the uneasiness. He responded with, "Don't worry, you won't get in trouble," which put

---

186 Raynes, Brent. "An Interview with Timothy Frick: Writer, Cryptozoologist, and an MIB Impersonator (who the MIB may have impersonated!)" *Alternate Perceptions Magazine.* Issue #151. Alternate Perceptions Magazine, Aug. 2010. Web. 08 Aug. 2017. http://mysterious-america.com/frickinterview.html

Gary on alert since he could have forgotten to fill out a leave slip with his unit. Usually, standard protocol required a person to fill out a leave slip whenever they were going to be out of the area, even if they weren't working during that time. Gary mentioned that lots of people in his unit didn't want to waste their vacation days, so many didn't even fill them out.[187] In this case, it might have been possible that he hadn't, either. Plus, at the time, he wore a sweater overtop of a military uniform, which did have his name, but he wasn't comfortable to reveal any information to a total stranger, just in case.

After Gary boarded the DC-10 aircraft bound for JFK, a second man with blonde hair sat in the seat on his immediate right. The man conversed with Gary about something, but again, he doesn't recall the specifics of what they talked about. As the plane filled up with passengers, the blonde-haired man was asked by the stewardess to leave since where he remained did not match the assigned seat on his ticket. So, the man got up and stood by the emergency exit door behind Gary and continued his conversation.

The stewardess came over a second time and asked the man to be seated in his correct seat, but he insisted to find out Gary's name for whatever reason before he left. Perhaps in an attempt to appease the man as well as the stewardess, Gary finally did reveal it, but the man didn't hear well and asked him to repeat it. Still uneasy about the whole affair, Gary opted not to, and the man left for his actual seat, which was further back in the plane. After the encounters, Gary had a strange feeling that maybe the men planned to break into his apartment. Between the two of them, they knew he'd be out of town for a few days. So, upon arrival in New York, Gary called his apartment manager to check up on the place while he was gone. Fortunately, his apartment was never broken into, but something more bizarre would soon take place instead.

That same day he arrived in New York, Gary and his father met with UFO investigator, Colman VonKeviczky, who was the former director of the Intercontinental UFO Research and Analytic Network, to discuss some of the sightings Gary's father and uncle saw previously in the area. VonKeviczky was one of the "unofficial spokesmen" for the UFO hearings held at the United Nations Special Political Committee on November 28, 1978. This was the one and only time such a presentation has ever been conducted for the U.N. on the UFO topic. VonKeviczky was a good friend with its organizer, the Prime Minister of Grenada, Sir Eric Gairy. The panel

187 Sudbrink, Gary. Phone interview. 09 Aug. 2016.

was also attended by such notables as astronaut Gordon Cooper, ufologist Leonard Stringfield, Dr. J. Allen Hynek (scientific advisor to Operation Blue Book), Dr. Jacques Vallee (French astronomer and computer scientist portrayed in Steven Spielberg's film *Close Encounters of the Third Kind*), and Lee Speigel (*Huffington Post* editor), just to mention a few. Unfortunately, in the spring the following year, Sir Eric Gairy, the main proponent of the hearings, was overthrown in a military coup, and the U.N. resolution was never looked at again.[188]

After returning from the meeting with VonKeviczky, Gary placed a call to his longtime friend, Mike Bagatta, who had no prior knowledge of him being in town—at least that's what Gary thought. It wasn't until he gave Mike a call that he discovered that Mike claimed he already spoke with Gary the previous day. According to what Mike told Gary, the impersonator sounded as if he had a stuffy nose and was coming down with a cold.[189]

Gary was shocked and didn't know what to make of it. Clearly it was not him who had called. In fact, the impersonator stated he had flown in through LaGuardia airport, when Gary had actually come in through JFK. As he got ready to end his phone call with Mike, another call came in, as indicated by the call waiting beep on the other line. Gary picked it up and his whole life changed from that moment on as a deep, mechanical voice greeted him on the line. Gary instinctively pressed record on the nearby answering machine to document it. My thoughts are that he wouldn't have done this had he not had the bizarre conversation with Mike just prior. Or perhaps it was in combination with the events that occurred earlier that day with his family's sightings.

At the time both his mother and father were present in the room.

Here is my original transcription of the first call already in progress after Gary pressed record...

Call #1 – Monday, February 08, 1993, 10:30 pm
Duration: 3 minutes, 46 seconds

---

188 Speigel, Lee. "WikiLeaks Documents Reveal United Nations Interest In UFOs." *HuffPost.* Oath/HuffPost/HPMG News, 29 Oct. 2016. Web. 09 Aug. 2017. http://www.huffingtonpost.com/entry/wikileaks-ufos-united-nations_us_5813aa17e4b0390e69d0322e

189 Sudbrink, Gary. Phone interview. 09 Aug. 2016.

GARY: I'll tell you who it is.
VOICE: Hello?

GARY: Yeah. Do you want to speak to him?

VOICE: Is Gary Sud–Sudbrink there?
GARY: Yeah, who's this? Steven? Are you playing games with me or what?

GARY: Huh? Steven if you're playing games here, I'm going to kick your ass.

VOICE: So how long are you going to be back from Texas?
GARY: Huh?

VOICE: You're being impersonated by the other voice.
GARY: Yeah this is you Steven—you idiot. You're pissing me off. Jerk. I'm gonna get you on...let's see what it says. Review. One new call. Out of area? Is Steven out of the area?

VOICE (interrupts): How long are you going to be back from Texas?
GARY: Wait, say that again.

VOICE: You're being impersonated by the other voice.
GARY: Wait, hold on. Is Steven out of the calling area or what?

MOM: How do I know?
GARY: What do you mean, you don't know? He's in Queens.
DAD: Well who are you talking to?
GARY: I don't know who the f*** I'm talking to...

VOICE (interrupts): Hello?
MOM: Hello?

VOICE: Is Gary Sud–Sudbrink there?

MOM: Who is this?
GARY (in background): Let me talk to him.

MOM: Somebody sounds like a robot.

GARY: Hello?
VOICE: How long are you going to be back from Texas?
GARY: What was that again, sir?

VOICE: You're being impersonated by the other voice.
GARY (to family): Oh be quiet—else, eh? Sorry, will you say that again?
GARY: Hello? I'm being impersonated by what voice?

VOICE: Hello?
GARY: Yeah. Hello?

VOICE: Is Gary Sud–Sudbrink there?
GARY: Yeah, hold on a second.
MOM: Who is that?
GARY: It's Steven. Okay. Yeah what is your question? I'll answer it.

DAD (in background): ...a strange voice.
VOICE: So how long are you going to be back from Texas?
GARY: How long--
VOICE (interrupts): You're being impersonated by the other voice.
GARY: Right. When am I coming back? Is that your question?

VOICE (quieter voice): Sudbrink there?
DAD (in background): What's a matter with you?
GARY: Okay there was a break, hold on. You wanna know when I'm coming back to Texas. Uh, is that your question?

VOICE: So how long are you going to be back from Texas?
GARY: How long am I going to be back from Texas...
VOICE (interrupts): You're being impersonated by the other voice.

GARY (talking overtop): ...that question doesn't even make any sense.

GARY: Okay. I'll be coming back eventually. Um...I can't tell you when. You should know that question—the answer to the question because you seem to know more about me than I do. You know what I'm saying?

DAD: Are you a...intergalactic...uh...person?

GARY: Are you a space alien?
DAD: Sounds like he hung up.

GARY: I can't believe this.
DAD: It's—he hung up Gary.

GARY: See if he comes back.
DAD: Alright, I'll hang up.

*(**Dial tone.**)*

GARY: Jesus Christ. Oh my God man. I'm calling Mike back.

*(**Two beeps on the dial pad.**)*

Gary has two brothers—Steven, who is one year older, and Brian, who is five years younger. At the moment he received the first call, Gary thought it was just Steven playing a prank. Steven was not known to be a prankster, yet there was another strange occurrence, which happened to involve both Steven and Gary a few years before the phone call. While en route to a wedding (also in Long Island) Steven saw Gary drive up alongside him, make weird faces to get his attention, and then just simply drive off. Even though Gary was in Long Island at that time, he didn't have a car to drive, let alone the car he was apparently spotted in by his brother—an exact same make and model of the very one that was parked at his residence in San Antonio at the time!

Return to the night of the strange phone call in 1993. A few minutes after the first phone call, the phone rang a second time. Gary pressed record soon after the mechanical voice was recognized...

Call #2 – Monday, February 08, 1993, 11:10 pm
Duration: 3 minutes, 40 seconds

GARY: What is your question?

*(**Unidentified beep**—From telephone or answering machine?)*

GARY: Yes, uh speaking.

VOICE: Is this Gary Sudbrink?
GARY: Yes.
GARY: Could I answer any questions for you?

VOICE: Are you back from Texas–ss?
GARY: I'm not back yet. No.

VOICE: How long are you going to be back from Texas?
GARY: Let me answer...first you tell me—where are you calling from?

VOICE: Is this Gary Sudbrink?
GARY: Yeah. Why don't you tell me where you're calling from?

VOICE: Who is this?
GARY: What do you mean who is this? You should know who it is. It's me, Gary.

GARY: Uhhh... Wait, let me...let me ask you this question. Where are you calling from?

GARY: Okay, I'll be back—
VOICE (interrupts): Keep an eye on the skies.
GARY: Excuse me?

VOICE: Near Orion.
GARY: I can't hear too well.

VOICE: The full moon.
GARY: Yeah there's a full moon out, that's true.

*(**Sound of someone hanging up on the other line.**)*

GARY: Could you identify yourself?

GARY: Identify yourself.
DAD: Ask him what's the purpose of the call.
GARY: Why are you calling me?
VOICE (interrupts): Keep an eye on the skies.
GARY: Excuse me?

VOICE: Near Orion.
GARY: I cannot hear too well.
DAD: Get on the other phone, it's better.
GARY: Hold on, let me switch phones.

*(**Sound of other phone being picked up.**)*

GARY: Okay. Okay hold on. Now who are you?

VOICE: Keep an eye on the skies.
GARY: Keep an eye on the sky he said.

DAD: Keep an eye on the sky?
GARY: Yeah.
VOICE: Orion.
DAD: Ask him can I talk to him--
GARY: ...shhh...shhh...
DAD: I had a sighting already--

GARY: ...okay, hold on. Say that...repeat that again?

GARY: Please repeat?

VOICE: Keep an eye on the skies.
GARY: Okay.
VOICE: Near Orion.

GARY: Near Orion.
DAD: Holy Mackerel. Tonight or this a when—
VOICE (interrupts): The full moon.
GARY: The full moon.

DAD (in background): They talk...they hung up...
VOICE: Show double of you.
DAD (in background): Keep an eye on the sky near Orion...

GARY: Repeat?

DAD: Tell him I'd like to talk to him.
GARY: Okay...repeat...repeat last word?

*(**Static on the telephone line.**)*

GARY: I'm hearing static.
DAD: Tell him I'd like to talk to him.

*(**Sound of caller disconnecting.**)*

GARY: He hung up.
DAD: He hung up?
GARY: Hello?

Gary related another time when he was a child in a Sizzler restaurant. He went to use the bathroom and another young boy came up and asked him if he was, in fact, Gary Sudbrink. Young Gary had never met the child before, nor had any reason to believe that he should have known him. Although he can't be sure that the event had actually taken place as he remembered, it still stands out as something unusual and one of his earliest recollections of high strangeness, in general.[190]

Later that same night in February of 1993, the strange caller phoned back a third time. Here is the transcription of that phone call, which was already in progress before Gary pressed the record button...

190 Sudbrink, Gary. Phone interview. 03 Sept. 2016.

Call #3 – Monday, February 08, 1993, 11:38 pm
Duration: 3 minutes, 33 seconds

GARY: Okay. Yeah, it's taking time for him to talk. Who is this?

*(**Sound of someone picking up the other line.**)*

GARY: Steven, I'm gonna—this is not funny you know.
VOICE (barely audible): Who is this?

DAD: Brian, it's not Steven.
GARY: What do you mean Brian?
DAD: I mean, uh...Gary.

GARY: How do I know it's not Steven?
DAD: It's not Steven.

DAD: Hello? I had a, uh...UFO experience in West Virginia, which you probably know. And I know that you're inter...uh... an intergalactic person.
VOICE (...very low, unintelligible...possibly "Who is this?")
DAD: Can you speak a little louder? Sir? Can you speak a little louder?
VOICE: (even lower...unintelligible...)
DAD: Louder?
GARY: Let me speak to him, Dad. I guess, I don't know…
DAD: Okay I'll hang up so you can talk to him. He wants to talk to you.
GARY: Okay.

*(**Sound of the other line hanging up.**)*

GARY: Hello? Can I help you?
VOICE (louder than before): Hello?
GARY: Yes.

VOICE: Is Gary Sudbrink there?
GARY: Yes, that's me.

VOICE (fainter again): Here is Gary Sudbrink.
GARY: Yes, could you please identify yourself?

GARY: Identify—
VOICE (faint, interrupts): Are you back from Texas–ss?
GARY: Yeah I'm back. I'm in Texas right now.

(**Sound of Gary's dad in the background.**)

GARY: Well, he asked me a question.
VOICE: (very low...unintelligible...possibly "How are long are you?")
GARY: No I'm in New York right now. You know that. Why are you asking me such a question?

DAD (in background): ...Assuming he's going to call back three times in a row, what are you going to do?

VOICE: Is this Gary Sudbrink?
GARY: Yes. Steven if this is you, I'm...I swear to God I'm gonna be pissed.

(**Sound of Gary's dad in the background.**)

VOICE: Who is this?
GARY: Huh?

(**Static on the line.**)

DAD (in background): It's not Steven.
GARY: I'm trying to listen to him. Who are...excuse me?
DAD (in background): You keep playing games with Steven and it's not Steven—
MOM (in background): Well, shut the hell up.

(**Intense static on the line.**)

GARY: Okay. Eventually I'll be back from Texas. Could you speak more? Please speak more.

*(**Intense static on the line.**)*

VOICE (barely audible): ...eye on the skies...

GARY: I guess it's not Steven. I believe it because I'm getting static.
DAD: Steven would not leave three times.
GARY: Let...let me go on this phone because I could never hear on this phone. Hold on.

*(**Sound of the other telephone line picked up, followed by a quick beep.**)*

GARY: Okay. Okay, please speak. Hello?

VOICE (louder than before, but still soft): Keep an eye on the skies.

*(**Sound of writing or scratching, followed by another quick beep.**)*

GARY: Okay, should I go out right now?
VOICE (interrupts): Orion.
GARY: Right now?

VOICE: The full moon.
GARY: Okay, see...I'm not sure where Orion is now, but we'll go outside.

VOICE: Show double from you.
GARY: It will show double from me?

*(**Static on the line.**)*

GARY: Repeat that again?

*(**Static on the line.**)*

*(**Caller hangs up.**)*

*(**Gary hangs up.**)*

That was the end of the mysterious phone calls on that specific night. But on February 9 (the next evening) the mechanical voice returned. Although his mother wasn't present for it, Gary, his father, and his Uncle Tom were.

Both his uncle and father were en route to visit the location of another strange incident back in 1988, where a radio tower collapsed at the Green Bank Observatory in West Virginia. They speculated that a UFO had possibly cut it down with a laser,[191] contrary to the official explanation—a sudden failure in a large gusset plate of the box girder assembly, a key structural element, which formed the main support for the antenna.[192] To verify their UFO suspicions, the two men attempted to meet with and speak to an employee at the observatory, but were unable to do so. However, in the midst of their travels they didn't leave empty-handed and instead ended up with an impressive UFO sighting of their own.

Now there's an interesting synchronicity that involves one of the major achievements of that particular telescope. It was the first to discover a helical magnetic field in interstellar space, coiled like a snake around a gas cloud in the constellation of Orion.[193] *Keep your eyes on the skies. Near Orion.*

Here is the transcript of the final call…

Call #4 – Tuesday, February 09, 1993, 10:21 pm
Duration: 3 minutes, 55 seconds

---

191 Sudbrink, Gary. Phone interview. 09 Aug. 2016.

192 "300-Foot Telescope Collapse." *National Radio Astronomy Observatory.* Associated Universities, 19 Sept. 2011. Web. 09 Aug. 2017. http://www.nrao.edu/whatisra/hist_300ft.shtml

193 Sanders, Robert. "Astronomers find magnetic Slinky in Orion." *UC Berkley News.* UC Regents, 12 Jan. 2006. Web. 09 Aug. 2017. http://www.berkeley.edu/news/media/releases/2006/01/12_helical.shtml

VOICE (with more reverb and echo): Is Gary Sudbrink there?
GARY: Yes, this is me. Can I speak to...can I ask why—
VOICE: Is Gary Sudbrink there?
GARY: Yes, can I ask why you're calling?

*(**Static on the line.**)*

GARY: Can I please ask—
VOICE: Is this Gary Sudbrink?
GARY: Yes, this is.

VOICE: Gary Sudbrink.
GARY: Yes, that is me.

*(**Static on the line.**)*

VOICE: We come. To be within this planet.
GARY: Say that again?

VOICE: In this planet.
GARY: Leave?

*(**Unknown sounds.**)*

VOICE: We come.
GARY: I'm standing right here.
VOICE: To be within this planet.
GARY: Is this a joke or what?

*(**A whirring sound on the line.**)*

VOICE: To visit the many. To be contacted. As the same. With you.

*(**Sound of door being shut in the background.**)*

GARY: Umm...

*(**Static and whirring sound on the line.**)*

GARY: I have to think about that. I'd like to see you—
VOICE (interrupts): To visit the many. To be contacted. As the same. With you.

UNCLE: Hey, let me tell you something. I've been listening to you. And I've had contacts with you.
VOICE: Beware. Government interference.
GARY: Government interference?

*(**Static on the line.**)*

VOICE (faint): You—
GARY: You have? Please explain what type of interference.

*(*Whirring sound on the line.**)*

VOICE: Beware.
GARY: Okay.
VOICE: Government interference. Visitations to be disrupted by them.

*(**Strange unidentified sound on the line.**)*

VOICE: (...unintelligible, faint...) ...appears. The sun will rise on...dark side of moon. World. Know.
UNCLE: The sun will rise...
VOICE: (...unintelligible...)
UNCLE: ..on the dark side of the moon?

GARY: Okay, umm...
VOICE (very low...unintelligible...maybe "on the moon")

GARY: What branch of the government?

*(**Intense static on the line.**)*

VOICE (very low): Show double from you.

*(**Intense static on the line.**)*

GARY: What uhh...what should I do?

*(**Intense static on the line.**)*

VOICE: Beware. Government interference. Visitations to be disrupted by them.
GARY: Okay. Is that good for me or bad?

*(**Caller disconnects the call.**)*

GARY: They hung up.
Dad (in background): So, did you get…?
UNCLE: Yes. Uh.

The argument could be made that the mysterious caller sounds just like—well, a recording. In other words, it could be that there was no intelligence behind the voice and that it was merely a disguised voice played on a loop. However, when I listened carefully to some of the calls, there were times when the patterns of the responses appear exactly the same, but at other times they differ slightly.

After I analyzed the particular tone and style of the calls, I soon discovered that there were seventeen instances of the unidentified voice in the first call, sixteen instances in the second, fifteen in the third, then back up to seventeen again in the fourth and final call on the second night. Perhaps the caller had lost energy as the calls progressed throughout that first night. The audible volume of the voice actually becomes much quieter. This is similar to how people commonly report conversations with MIB-type entities. Gary believed these calls to be such examples of that too.[194]

The other thing worth noting is how mechanical the voice itself was. This would also match up with other reports of encounters with MIB in their tone and nature. People often report these entities as very mechanical or robotic, leading some researchers to consider if they are even intelligent entities at all, or just drones of some sort, perhaps under control by another separate, unseen presence.

194 Sudbrink, Gary. Phone interview. 09 Aug. 2016.

Timothy Frick also agrees with the possibility that the MIB could be artificial beings, similar to a robot or android, but a lot more complex. However, one thing is for sure, they're devious enough to enjoy toying with the human race. Frick further thinks that the MIB operate outside of our reality, and somehow know when certain events will occur before they actually happen, thus giving them this precognitive advantage over us.[195]

It is seldom reported, but sometimes abductees (and even those involved with the research) have received these types of strange calls, like the ones I mentioned earlier with Marie and Anna in California. To Gary's knowledge, he does not consider himself an abductee, nor is he aware of any events related to what is commonly reported in the abduction scenario.

195 Frick, Timothy. Correspondences conducted via electronic messaging. 09 Aug. 2017.

"I don't think we're at the point of asking the right questions. I think that what we have is so terribly complex that it is beyond our imagination. And that when we attempt to do research projects, it's almost laughable."[196]

– Dr. John Alexander (Col., Retired)

196 "Dr. John Alexander, The Mysterious Skinwalker Ranch." *Open Minds UFO Radio.* Open Minds Production/Blog Talk Radio, 11 Oct. 2016.

The Elusive Nature of It All

The tired question is often posed—*If UFOs exist then why don't they just land on the White House lawn?*

But this is under the presumption that the agenda of those behind the spectrum actually *want* to reveal themselves. However, in July of 1952 they came close to the White House lawn as objects were tracked over restricted airspace above Washington, which put the military on high alert.

Is contact truly part of the visitors' agenda? We can't say for sure, as there just isn't enough evidence to conclusively support the notion. Yet there's not enough evidence to point to the contrary, either. In some ways contact has been made, if you take into consideration the vast number of abductees, contactees, mass sightings, and UFO flaps that have been reported all over the world. But in other ways contact has not been made, since no governmental body has officially come out to say it either. To date, all we have are government studies like AATIP (Advanced Aerospace Threat Identification Program), made public in 2017. But all that showed was that *something* inexplicable is around us, yet the motives behind that something remain just as inexplicable.

A pattern that's evident within the spectrum is its sheer evasiveness to leave humanity with any solid answers whatsoever.

In Gary Sudbrink's experiences there was another interesting event, which took place long before he ever received those bizarre phone calls. It occurred outside of his apartment complex in San Antonio, Texas when he first took note of the distinct sound of helicopter blades cutting through the air. As he slid open the patio doors to take a look there was indeed a massive chopper over an undeveloped plot of land that bordered the apartment parking lot. But this helicopter hovered just twenty feet above the ground! All it took was Gary to turn away for a couple of seconds, in order to retrieve his eyeglasses for a closer inspection, and the helicopter had completely vanished.

At the same time, there was another tenant who had been outside washing his car directly across from the incident. In the moment, Gary thought he should have asked the man to verify what had taken place, but instead opted not to. He said, "It would seem so ridiculous (to ask him) because how could you not see it? It was like lightning hitting the neighbor's house and people standing around watching it and you asking if they've seen it. It just seemed so stupid of a question to ask him, so I didn't."[197] As he reflected back on the incident, Gary actually regretted not asking. Should we consider the possibility that the phenomenon could have subtly influenced him in that moment in order to preserve its covert nature?

Consider Gary's reflections on the conversations he had with the two men at the airport, before he flew home and received those strange phone calls. How is it that he can recall so much detail about the events surrounding the two men, yet hardly recall any details about the actual conversations he had with them to begin with? Gary speculated that it could have been because the conversations were so mundane,[198] but then we must also ask why the two men were so intent on uncovering his identity to begin with. Wouldn't Gary have had at least a general idea why they were so obsessed with him? Yet strangely he cannot remember their exact intentions or why they seemed so uninterested in the other people at the airport.

This amnesia-like effect, which seems to be present in various aspects throughout the experience in general, could be a common thread that warrants further study. I encourage the investigator today to not just examine the more dramatic aspects of the experiences, but also the seemingly insignificant ones too. We need to document not just the events, but also how the witnesses *respond* to the events. There could be equally impressive data contained within their thought patterns and behaviors, which provide additional insight into how the phenomenon works to

197 Sudbrink, Gary. Phone interview. 03 Sept. 2016.

198 Sudbrink, Gary. Phone interview. 09 Aug. 2016.

maintain its elusiveness. The same forces may be more manipulative than we realize.

Over the summer of 2017, I interviewed my mother to talk about the supernatural aspects of the house I grew up in. When we shifted gears to talk about this very concept of manipulating forces within the spectrum, she abruptly brought up an unrelated online video she had seen. This had absolutely no connection to the conversation we were in the middle of. When I stopped her to inquire, she looked at me as if an unseen hand had pulled the rug out from underneath our prior conversation. A look of genuine concern came over her as she was left with no explanation for it. And of course, I had turned off my pocket recorder just prior to the moment too. The phenomena must know it's being observed as it observes us.

David Jacobs discusses a telepathic ability demonstrated by these alien beings as influencing thoughts and "switching off" bystanders during an abduction experience.[199] If those entities have that kind of power, then what's stopping similar forces within the spectrum from using additional tactics to further maintain its covert presence?

Manipulative characteristics exist within the Djinn—a mischievous character of Arabian mythology and Islamic theology. Rosemary Ellen Guiley has tackled the subject more in-depth and considers them to be one of the root causes of many, if not all of the supernatural activity on this planet.[200] The Djinn are believed to exist everywhere but like to remain hidden in order to preserve their elusiveness. It is also thought that if the Djinn discover that a researcher is hot on the trail of their existence in one form or another, they can even persuade the person to give up that research.

Yet it's the unpredictability of the phenomena, which makes it difficult for science to accept, let alone test, control, or repeat in a lab environment. These forces do not seem to "fit" within the framework of our standard scientific principles. And if these forces operate outside of those principles then we would be quite naïve to believe they would play by our standard rules of logic too. These extra-, inter-, or ultra-terrestrials

---

199 Jacobs, David M., PhD. "Abductees, Aliens, and the Program—The Abduction Process." *Walking Among Us: The Alien Plan to Control Humanity*. Kindle ed., Disinformation Books-Red Wheel/Weiser, 2015. pg. 36.

200 Guiley, Rosemary E. "The Long Shadow of the Djinn." Main Line MUFON Monthly Speaker Series. Tredyffrin Library, Wayne. 12 May 2015. Lecture.

appear to neither be good nor bad. To think that the dichotomy of a black and white world applies to the world in which they emanate from detracts us from understanding why they are even here in the first place. Whether their motives are considered good or bad, their track record has displayed them to be master deceivers in how we respond to their presence.

The transformative effect of the alien abduction is a significant indicator of this. In the beginning of the abduction experience, an abductee is generally terrified of their encounter. Yet, as they come to terms with this ongoing intrusion, which generally continues throughout the majority of their life, they may find themselves oddly at peace with it. Some abductees may even sympathize with their kidnappers, eventually regarding them as enlightened beings with a misunderstood kindness as they attempt to save humanity from destruction. But this is merely the information (or disinformation) they are provided, perhaps to help process and rationalize such a traumatizing experience at its core. Not to mention that there is the conscious recollection of the experience itself, which has been manipulated also. Several abductees have what are referred to as screen memories—these being vivid, irrelevant events that could actually mask the abduction experience itself.[201]

Problems with Technology Amidst a Covert Presence

In a modern era where technology is in every hand and home, one would expect to find more convincing evidence of the phenomenon, yet that hardly seems to be the case. What seems more evident is our unsatisfied reception to the data that is there—the best evidence is too good while the rest is never good enough. Will there ever be something that both the believers and skeptics equally desire? It's highly unlikely if that middle of the road, smoking gun, piece of proof is more like a thin strand in which we're trying to balance an elephant on.

Not to mention our presumption that the phenomenon actually wants to be documented in the first place. A great example was in April of 1950,

201 Jacobs, David M., PhD. "Abductees and Their Testimony—Skeptics, Debunkers, and the Facts and Hand." *Walking Among Us: The Alien Plan to Control Humanity.* Kindle ed., Disinformation Books-Red Wheel/Weiser, 2015. pg. 13.

when the U.S. Air Force began a one-year study called "Project Twinkle." This was an exploration into mysterious green fireballs that appeared over the skies of New Mexico and virtually all of the state's top-secret military facilities. They attempted to photograph the phenomenon, but it simply moved to another location, almost as if it didn't want its picture taken at all.[202] Those green fireballs are still observed to this day.

Author and investigator Mark O'Connell wrote about a more recent example, which involved a truck driver who had gone out to Lucky Point, Indiana—an area known for numerous paranormal and UFO encounters—to test out a brand new infrared camera. The man took several pictures of the area's landscape to test how the night-vision setting responded to the daylight, then switched off the camera, slipped it back into his shirt pocket and hiked back to his car. When he reached his car, he suddenly felt like someone was standing right beside him, even though he was completely alone. He called his wife in the moment while the camera turned itself on and deleted the pictures that he had taken, one by one. The wife verified she heard the camera click and beep repeatedly the whole time they were on the phone. Since the man had not kept track of the total amount of photos he had in the first place, he had no idea how many exactly had been deleted. However, a few photos were left untouched.[203] Is this an example of the unseen attempting to stay covert, or merely a case of someone lacking proper technological expertise?

I've heard of similar things, which also happen to UFO witnesses, alien abductees and paranormal investigators in attempts to document their experiences. This should come as no surprise again in the face of something that attempts to conceal its presence most of the time. However, the important thing to keep in mind is our general tendency (or to some, wishful thinking) for the strange to be the usual suspect in each and every instance. Just because we're dealing in the topic of high strangeness doesn't give us the right to automatically assign blame to it whenever something seemingly inexplicable does occur.

In the spring of 2010, I consulted with a man about a series of seemingly paranormal events that took place inside his home. The classic

---

202 *UFOs: The Best Evidence 2: The Government Cover-Up*. Directed by George Knapp & Bryan Gresh, Altamira Broadcast, 1994.

203 O'Connell, Mark. "Lucky Point, Indiana." *High Strangeness*. Blogger, 15 Jan. 2012. Web. 18 Aug. 2017. http://www.highstrangenessufo.com/2012/01/lucky-point-indiana.html

symptoms of a haunting were reported over the span of a few weeks—from disembodied voices to shadowy presences to things being moved from one spot to another as he slept. Things came to a point of dire concern for him however when a package left on his front porch one evening appeared on his kitchen stove the following morning.

Perhaps there was something mystical about the contents of the package since the man had an interest in collecting vintage items. Initially I thought there was a lingering entity or energy attached to something he brought home as one possibility. He was reluctant to reveal the contents of the package to me, but I continued to press him for it. After he did, a startling conclusion soon took form. The cause of the incredible abilities bestowed upon the package to either open doors or simply pass through them, wasn't found in the contents per se, but rather in the altered state of its beholder. Inside were the contents of marijuana, which the man had left for one of his friends to pick up the previous evening. Much to his surprise, the correlation between being high and the "haunting" was evident once a prescribed antidote of staying sober for the next week cleared up any such activity from further taking place. He eventually reverted back to his old habits later on once he moved from that particular house.

But not all instances of the paranormal can be easily dismissed, including those with seemingly common technical disruptions. In the well-documented 1989 San Pedro, California poltergeist case, Jackie Hernandez (the target of the haunting) made a frantic phone call to principal investigators Barry Conrad and Dr. Barry Taff. In the midst of their call, the line was disconnected and then reconnected a few moments later.[204] Electronic malfunctions seem to be a common occurrence with other investigators I've spoken to, especially those who have worked on the more intense cases involving poltergeists, negative entities, or the demonic. I've experienced similar interference or had calls abruptly cut at pivotal points when simply just discussing such things over the phone. Maybe it's not a malevolent force that is responsible for the interference so much as it could be further evidence of stress-induced psychokinetic discharge (SIPD) that I mentioned earlier.

In 2011, a couple in Pemberton, New Jersey contacted me for an investigation soon after they purchased a home there as part of an estate sale. The property belonged to an elderly man who passed away just prior.

---

204 *An Unknown Encounter: A True Account of the San Pedro Haunting.* Directed by Barry Conrad. BarCon, 1997.

He didn't have any family to will his belongings to, so the new couple just inherited it as part of the sale. The woman attempted to document some of the paranormal activity to show me that she wasn't crazy. But her attempt was met with an unexpected surprise. The several-minutes-long video she thought she had recorded of a flashlight switching on and off turned out to be just three *seconds* of unimpressive footage. What happened to the rest of the video? Was it just another instance of user error, or an eerie invisible edit? Even though the video she sent wasn't the documented evidence we had both hoped, it added credibility to other events both her and her husband experienced consistent with a presence able to directly affect electronic devices, especially in the kitchen.

So, I set up a small team to conduct an investigation over the course of two back-to-back nights. Although we logged several hours at the property, the most memorable moment took place within the first hour of setting up. As I instructed investigator Tim Schmidt to turn off the lights in the house, he asked if I wanted the outside porch light off too.

Unbeknownst at the time, an audio recorder on the kitchen table in front of Tim, where the woman had attempted to document her experience, picked up a direct response to Tim's question that night—a single word, "never" in a clear male voice. This was immediately followed by two flashlights next to the recorder that proceeded to roll off the table and onto the floor. But what I find particularly interesting is the strange electronic feedback picked up during the recording, which immediately preceded the flashlights first beginning to roll and then repeated a second time after they landed on the hard kitchen floor. The feedback or voice wasn't picked up by any of the other video cameras or audio recorders.

Another tie-in to this otherworldly interference exhibited by the phenomenon is the phantom phone calls or apparent voice messages from the dead. After attending the 2016 East Coast Paracon in Scranton, Pennsylvania, a woman in the audience relayed one particular experience that involved an eerie message left on her answering machine after her brother-in-law passed.

She hadn't been very fond of her brother-in-law, not only because of his drug problem, but because he was not a nice man, according to her description. His addiction got the best of him and a fatal overdose got the rest of him. A couple of weeks after the funeral, she discovered a message that had been left for her and her husband on their answering machine. The message merely said, "Come with me." She instantly recognized the voice as that of the now deceased brother-in-law, which was also later confirmed by her husband when he listened to it. According to the woman, her husband was so disturbed by the message that he acknowledged it, but immediately discounted it.

At the conference the woman posed the question, "Why had it been me that was asked to come with him?"

Rosalyn Lewis was also present that day and offered the following explanation to the woman: "Because your reaction was not like that of your husband's. Perhaps this is why your brother-in-law chose to leave the message with you, instead of him."

Those who don't buy into the possibility of this so-called nonsense may secretly desire an experience to change their minds, as it were. It seems to be a wish rarely granted however, as the unseen seems more drawn to those already open and accepting of it to start. The other side, whatever side it originates from—whether within us or beyond—seems to know who to connect with and how to connect with them in order to both draw near to and remain at a distance from, simultaneously. Presumably out of fear, the woman immediately disposed of the tape that had her brother-in-law's voice. A wise decision on her part perhaps on the off chance that something else could have masked itself as her brother-in-law. We cannot be guaranteed that anything, whether an image, a voice or just a simple impression of someone familiar, is something we should completely trust as such, especially at face value.

What We Think We Know and How Little We Do Know

The trickster aspect as a whole is something we tend to often overlook. Whether this is unintentional (or intentional on the trickster's part) we'd like to think we have more control over *it,* but *it* just as easily assumes subtle control over us! We are completely oblivious to how the different representations of the phenomena operate—not just in a present time circumstance, but also a future one—so it would appear that the phenomena also have an ability to stay one step ahead of us.

In the Skinwalker Ranch case for example, the activity there displayed a sort of cyclical pattern. In the years where the NIDS team was involved, they discovered windows of intense activity on the ranch followed by extended periods of no activity whatsoever. The NIDS team instrumented the ranch with full-time monitoring twenty-four hours, yet, even still, the phenomena had the ability to function just outside of wherever they had placed the monitoring equipment and sensors. Dr. John Alexander, who investigated and witnessed this elusive aspect first-hand, refers to it as a precognitive sentient phenomenon...

> *"Certainly, this was one of the more highly concentrated areas and one in which you had this variety of phenomena that were occurring and defying scientific explanation and attempts to do research. Hence, it was a precognitive sentient phenomenon. It knew what we were going to do. It seemed to know how we would respond and what kinds of research we would attempt to do and yet present things that were ineffable. It's in charge. Whatever it is, it is in charge. That may be one of the more scary aspects."*[205]

For example, Alexander stated that there were four twenty-foot poles looking to the west with surveillance cameras positioned on top. In addition to these cameras, there were several cameras to the east that were in perfect sight of the west-facing cameras to make sure that the entire field being monitored was covered. These cameras were attached with half a roll of duct tape holding the wires in place that led up from the ground to the top of the pole. A combination of PVC pipes and U-clamps held the wires in place where they traveled underground to a separate building that displayed the live video feed.[206]

At one point, one of the cameras further to the west stopped recording at the same time its respective camera to the east stopped recording. The wires at the top of the twenty-foot pole were pulled loose, along with the PVC holding the U-clamps in place at the bottom being pulled out. In addition, a yard-long chunk of wire had inexplicably gone missing, almost as if it had been cut out, but it was just gone. And yet nothing was documented on the camera system. Alexander said that if there had been something normal such as a human element that had caused it, the cattle

---

205 "Dr. John Alexander, The Mysterious Skinwalker Ranch." *Open Minds UFO Radio.* Open Minds Production/Blog Talk Radio, 10 Oct. 2016.

206 "Dr. John Alexander, The Mysterious Skinwalker Ranch." Open Minds UFO Radio. Open Minds Production/Blog Talk Radio, 10 Oct. 2016.

would've scattered from the scene, but they were undisturbed and calm as if nothing had even taken place.[207]

Researchers refer to places like Skinwalker Ranch as portals or "window areas." With these apparent hot spots, though they display high strangeness in one category, they will often also come bundled with aspects of strangeness in other categories too. The same can be said for those people that the phenomena center around.

Pevely, Missouri resident Dan D. Doty, (no known relation to Richard Doty) is someone who has experienced a plethora of strange occurrences that do not stay neatly contained within one supernatural box. Like so many with Asperger syndrome (which Dan is diagnosed with), an individual can become intently focused on one particular thing and hone in on it. For Dan, it was a series of encounters with the ever-elusive Bigfoot, which became the catalyst for his journey towards becoming a paranormal "expert," in order to learn as much as he could about the things he experienced. But as he would come to realize, the topic itself often leads to more questions than the answers can ever provide.

There have been some inexplicable paranormal and precognitive experiences early in Dan's life that are interesting to note. When he was only six years of age, he remembers something materialize in his living room— "It looked like *The Hideous Sun Demon* wearing a trench coat" as he described it.[208] This was a 1959 science-fiction horror film depicting a creature that looked like a cross between *The Creature from the Black Lagoon, The Wolfman* and the classic "reptilian" described in numerous alien abduction reports. What this creature's intentions were or what the point of the apparition was to begin with however, was never made clear to him.

When Dan was around twelve years of age, he had a particularly interesting precognitive experience at his elementary school. Classes had just let out for the day when he saw two schoolmates walk from behind the school building and onto the parking lot. Then they suddenly vanished before Dan's eyes. A few moments later, the same two kids passed by him again, but this time he confronted them—

"Hey, didn't you two just pass by here already?" he asked. But the two kids just looked at him like he was crazy and continued on their way to

---

207 "Dr. John Alexander, The Mysterious Skinwalker Ranch." *Open Minds UFO Radio.* Open Minds Production/Blog Talk Radio, 10 Oct. 2016.

208 Doty, Dan. Phone interview. 22 March 2017.

the parking lot, exactly like Dan had seemingly already observed moments prior.

On December 4, 1980, Dan had a random thought pop into his head out of the blue as he sat at his kitchen table—*Gee, I wonder what would happen if one of The Beatles was dead?* Four days later, Mark David Chapman killed John Lennon on the streets of New York City. Nothing like that ever happened to Dan again until much later in 2009 while employed at a Walmart in Arnold, Missouri. As he cleaned up trash from the parking lot, another random thought shot into his head in the same manner—What if mom got cancer? A couple days later, his mother told him that she had a tumor in one of her lungs.

Dan was in his mid-twenties when a series of events took place that really attracted his attention. He and two friends, Daryl and Cliff, found themselves deep in the woods of Otto, Missouri at about midnight in September of 1987. They were in pursuit of rumors that locals and even law enforcement had encountered a Bigfoot-type creature in their neighborhood. During their trek, the three men came across a clearing and Daryl suggested how it would be a great place to play *Wacky Warriors*—a regional form of entertainment that combines paintball and laser tag. But movement in the trees quickly diverted them from their recreational aspirations.

As they aimed their flashlights towards the movement, they quickly discovered what it was—an extremely large bipedal creature violently shaking one of the nearby trees. Although it certainly fit the description of what they were after, it proved more than what they could handle, and Dan's two friends fled in fear, leaving Dan to himself and presumably for dead. As Dan stood there for a minute or so in awe of the creature, he decided to walk away casually, contrary to what his friends had done. Sure, it seemed abnormal at the time in comparison, but staying calm may have saved his life from whatever was out there—bear or Bigfoot.

Dan soon met back up with his two cowardly friends at another guy's house named Ace who lived next to the woods. Daryl and Cliff were still shaken up, but Ace had the suspicion that something may have followed them back. He went back outside with a high-powered Maglite and aimed it into the woods to see if his suspicions were correct. To his amazement he spotted a large creature with amber-colored eyes, which closed its eyes as soon as he shone the light on it. All of the men went back into the woods shortly after to see if they could catch another glimpse of the creature but came up empty handed.

Two weeks later, Dan returned to the woods next to Ace's house, but this time by himself and not in the middle of the night. It was closer to sunset but there was still enough light in the sky to provide a clear path, and probably a safer one. Although it wasn't a particularly exciting excursion overall, there was a bizarre point when suddenly everything in the woods became silent. "No bird, no squirrels, no insects. Everything was just dead quiet," he said.[209] The sudden deafening of sound, known as the *Oz effect,* is also reported in some UFO and MIB reports too. In some stranger instances, humans and animals will abruptly depopulate a busy location, only to reemerge once the phenomenon associated with it has left or ended.[210]

When Dan decided to look for the creature a third time it was with Ace on October 10, 1987. He remembers that night vividly because they had just finished an episode of *Star Trek: The Next Generation* and were amped to head back out into the unknown. The time was again approaching midnight when they ventured into the woods armed with high-powered flashlights and a renewed courage to boldly go where no man had gone before.

In the woods, Dan caught something that moved past him—he immediately shined his flashlight on the shape of a creature, which instantly froze in its place. It remained completely still as Dan held the light in place and took a closer look. He wondered if what he caught wasn't just part of a tree yet realized that there was too much detail in it—it was a face! He took his flashlight off the spot for just a second after being startled by Ace, but when he turned back the creature was gone. Dan says that the most accurate representation to what he saw was later found in the illustrations of Frank Frazetta. He said that he (Frazetta) got it exactly right.[211]

Dan and Ace followed down the path where they thought the creature had gone. They had made it only about twenty feet when Ace stopped suddenly. He was white as a sheet. "I just felt like I walked over my own grave," he explained to Dan. The sound of movement then surrounded the two of them, so they shined their flashlights in opposite directions. Dan

---

209 Doty, Dan. Phone interview. 22 March 2017.

210 Beckley, Timothy Green, et al. *Curse of the Men in Black: Return of the UFO Terrorists.* Global Communications, 2010. pg. 195.

211 Doty, Dan. Phone interview. 22 March 2017.

didn't catch anything from his side, but Ace shouted back, "It's as big as a house!"

The two men ran from the woods in sheer terror towards the safety of the roadside when they heard a horrifying, high-pitch scream, like a woman had just been stabbed. They then heard not just one, but two of these creatures communicate back and forth after that. Dan explained that the chatter was similar to the well-known "Sierra Sounds," a set of recordings made in the 1970s by researchers Ron Morehead and Al Berry in the Sierra Nevada Mountains of eastern California. Those recordings are regarded as some of the most convincing pieces of Bigfoot vocalizations to date. Dan mentioned that what he heard with Ace was similar but not quite as agitated as what appeared to be captured in those recordings.[212]

But to make matters even stranger, the men then witnessed a big, blue ball of light come down from the sky and into the woods towards the direction of where the creatures remained. Dan admits that this aspect eventually changed his perspective on what the creatures could be and opened up the possibility that perhaps they (Bigfoot) could be connected to them (UFOs). Dan also noted that within three to four months following this incident a large transmitter tower was erected in the same wooded region, in which he described the construction as very quick, almost as if it just "sprang up" suddenly.

Indeed, it was following these events that prompted Dan to pursue his interest in the paranormal full force, yet it wasn't until about ten years later when things began to get really intense for him. "I didn't have to look anymore, because the weird things were starting to come to me," he said.[213] There were extended periods when things would frequently happen followed by extended periods when absolutely nothing would happen. Doesn't that often seem to be the case with these UFO flaps and pockets of high strangeness, in general?

In 1997, Dan was waiting for his friend Terry to get takeout from the Shoney's Restaurant located in Arnold, MO, when a red car pulled up to him in the parking lot. An older Caucasian man with dark thinning hair stepped out of the vehicle, dressed in black casual clothes and carrying a traditional 35mm camera. The man snapped a series of quick photographs of Dan, then without hesitation, hopped back in the car and took off. Dan mentioned that all this occurred within such a close proximity that he

212 Doty, Dan. Phone interview. 22 March 2017.

213 Doty, Dan. Phone interview. 22 March 2017.

could even hear the camera's shutter going off. What in the world do these phantom photographers seem to be concerned with in regard to witnesses to strange phenomena?

Return of the Photographers and the Enigma of the Helicopters

As if that wasn't daunting enough, a series of hang-up phone calls to Dan Doty's residence for the next several years would ensue. The caller would wait for him to pick up the phone then immediately disconnect without ever uttering a word. In a lighter period, it was seven or eight calls a day, and in a heavier period—ten to twenty.

At that time, a person could simply dial *69 from their landline and it would automatically call back the last number that had called them. But this technique would never seem to work quite as well as Dan had hoped it would. Instead, he was connected with a previous caller who had called—but not necessarily the caller who had phoned him just prior to the *69 technique. In other words, Dan might have been connected with somebody who had called much earlier in the day, or in weeks prior, or even years prior. When he later installed the Caller ID feature on his phone, it further confirmed that they were in fact physical calls, even though the display would label them as unknown calls.

In 1997 Dan had worked the appropriately titled "graveyard shift" for a gas station and convenience store in Arnold, Missouri. As he came home one August morning, he spotted a black (or dark gray) unmarked helicopter that hovered a mere thirty feet off the ground in the vacant lot on his property. It was so close that Dan was able to see a Caucasian man through the open door of the helicopter pointing some sort of device at him. Even though Dan could identify the man's mustache and dark hair, he couldn't quite make out the device the man held but mentioned that it may have been a large lens camera. The helicopter remained in place for a period of about ten to fifteen seconds before it left.

What I find highly peculiar about this event is again, the subtle and often overlooked aspects involved. For example, it wasn't until Dan parked his car, then looked over towards the lot, that he suddenly took note of the aircraft. He does not remember hearing any sounds associated with the helicopter's entry or exit. This is highly unusual for a vehicle that is normally quite loud, especially a proximity where he can spot the individual inside of it. "I just turned around and there it was," as he recalled the experience.[214]

The next time something of a similar nature happened was around three weeks later at approximately 4:00 pm, when not just one, but two military-style Apache helicopters hovered over his residence. Again, the helicopters were so low that they just barely missed coming into contact with the nearby telephone poles. They angled up and took off soon after he caught sight of them. Dan noted that one of his neighbors, an older woman named Ellen, had also seen them, but she went back inside of her house as if it was nothing remarkable. Like in the case of Gary Sudbrink (who had also encountered a helicopter hover at low altitude, along with one of his neighbors), Dan was not inclined to discuss it with his neighbors, either.

This aspect of disinterest in the moment appears to be a commonality in these phantom helicopter reports. For whatever reason, people do not seem to discuss the events with their neighbors or even display much interest in the moments they occur. I would imagine that it is natural to look to validation from others if an event seems unusual or out of place. For example, when authorities suddenly converge on a neighborhood, this will no doubt bring out people to congregate and speculate as to what is taking place. Yet in the reports of extremely close helicopters being observed, the opposite occurs. Witnesses are even quite amazed at how disinterested they seemed to be when they look back on their experiences in hindsight.

"Why didn't I go approach my neighbor?" Southampton, New Jersey resident Marcia Moore told me after she too encountered one of these low-altitude helicopters.[215] Marcia arrived home from work to see it hovering just over her house, but she didn't hear it come in, either. She just looked up and there it was. One of her neighbors crossed the street as she took note of it, but just continued on her way as if nothing abnormal was present at all.

The incident took place after Marcia witnessed some bizarre light anomalies in the sky over the same region. There were certainly a lot of reports over that area in late 2016 and early 2017. Perhaps the phantom helicopters are connected to or even part of the UFO phenomenon in some way. In 1968-69, there was a UFO flap that occurred in Vietnam, and those sightings correlated with numerous reports of phantom helicopters too.[216]

---

214 Doty, Dan. Phone interview. 22 March 2017.

215 Moore, Marcia. Personal interview. 01 April 2017.

216 Keel, John A. *The Mothman Prophecies.* 1975. New York: Tor Books, 2002. pg. 36.

Dan mentioned seeing a 1980 article in *Life Magazine* where two women sued the federal government after they saw Chinook choppers trail a UFO that left burn marks on their bodies, following their close encounter. The Cash-Landrum incident is one of the few UFO cases to result in civil court proceedings. On December 29, 1980, Dayton, Texas residents Betty Cash and Vickie Landrum, along with Vickie's seven-year-old grandson Colby, drove home one evening and came across an intensely glowing, diamond-shaped object that hovered above the treetops in Piney Woods. The object emitted such intense heat that all three individuals suffered effects similar to that from radiation poisoning.

The date of this incident occurred ironically just one day after the last in a series of incidents with U.S. military personnel at RAF Bentwaters near Rendlesham Forest. The encounter with a UFO, or UAP (Unidentified Aerial Phenomenon) as it's also referred to as in official Ministry of Defence documents, also left adverse health effects on Airman First Class John Burroughs. He had served on base at the time and was one of the primary witnesses to the events in Rendlesham. His exposure to the phenomenon brought about various heart problems which he was finally able to get treatment for in 2015 after a long legal battle with the U.S. government to get the necessary coverage. However, to date, Burroughs' medical records are still classified for whatever reason.[217]

Since Cash and Landrum had also seen a plethora of helicopters both surrounding the object and escorting it out of the area, they theorized there must have been some sort of military involvement. There were 23 helicopters to be exact according to Betty, yet 26 counted by Vickie.[218] Detective Lamar Walker with the Dayton police claimed that he and his wife also took note of 12 Chinook-type helicopters near the same area at roughly the same time. But they did not report ever seeing the large diamond-shaped object that Cash and Landrum saw.[219] The women had brought upon a $20 million lawsuit in U.S. district court, which a judge

217 Rojas, Alejandro. "Vet says government has acknowledged he was injured by UFO while on duty." *Open Minds.* Open Minds Production. 03 Mar. 2015. Web. 09 Sept. 2017. http://www.openminds.tv/vet-says-government-acknowledged-injured-ufo-duty/32397

218 Klotz, Jim. "Transcript of Bergstrom AFB Interview of Betty Cash, Vickie & Colby Landrum, August 1981." *CUFON.* The Computer UFO Network. 04 June 1996. Web. 05 May 2017. http://www.cufon.org/cufon/cashlani.htm

219 World Heritage Encyclopedia. "Cash-Landrum Incident." *World Library.* World Library Foundation/World Public Library Association. Web. 05 May 2017. http://www.worldlibrary.org/articles/cash-landrum_incident

dismissed in 1986 on the basis that they had not proved they were U.S. government helicopters, along with the military's testimony that they did not possess a large, diamond-shaped aircraft in their arsenal, either.[220]

In the winter of 1998, a third incident involving a phantom helicopter took place with Dan, just before dusk. Behind his house was a large thirty-three-acre wooded area of completely undeveloped land. When the foliage was gone he could see a nice-sized field about the size of two basketball courts. As he passed by the living room window that evening a sight took him completely by surprise—a black helicopter hovered just three feet off the ground in front of his house. The first words out of his mouth were rather profane as he stood there in awe. Yet as soon as Dan saw that they saw him, the helicopter took off.

He didn't recall any sound either, which he also finds odd reflecting back on the incident now. Perhaps these black helicopters have now replaced the Men in Black, he suggested. It's an intriguing thought, given how these helicopters show up above people's houses instead of showing up on their doorstep.

Chosen for Something

After the first helicopter incident, an encounter of a different origin took place for Dan in Milwaukee, Wisconsin. Out of all his experiences, he considers this, by far, his strangest. It took place in August of 1995 at an event known as Gen Con, one of the largest annual tabletop game conventions. At the time, he and his friends were really into *Dungeons and Dragons*, so the convention was an ideal place to attend, network and game. During the event there were several other discussion groups that took place involving many different types of subjects, and not just ones centered on games. One of them was with individuals that had either encountered the alien abduction scenario in one form or another or those that considered themselves contactees. Dan decided to sit in on the discussion because of his general interest in the topic overall.

When he arrived back at the hotel room he had been sharing with two of his friends, he found himself quite exhausted, despite their enthusiasm to

220 World Heritage Encyclopedia. "Cash-Landrum Incident." *World Library*. World Library Foundation/World Public Library Association. Web. 05 May 2017. http://www.worldlibrary.org/articles/cash-landrum_incident

play Dungeons and Dragons in the separate next-door room. Dan politely refused so he could head to bed, much earlier than usual for him. He had been accustomed to staying up all night with his friends then catching up on sleep in the daytime, so this was a deviation from his typical schedule, given that it was only about 10:30 pm.

After he entered his bedroom, Dan switched the air conditioner on high, settled into bed, and almost immediately felt a presence enter the room, which he thought was one of his friends there to retrieve something. Dan sat up in bed expecting to see his friend Barry, but instead was greeted by a ring of light with a solid circle in the center of it. The light hovered directly above the foot of his bed with another beam of light that emitted out of the circle of light. He doesn't know why, but he reached out and grabbed the beam with his hand. When that happened he heard a voice, not audibly or telepathically in his head, but rather as he described it as emanating from where the "third eye"* is thought to exist.[221]

*This is an area directly above the eyes, above the bridge of the nose in the space between the eyebrows.

The voice told him, *"We will take you wherever you want to go."*

Dan replied, "I don't want to go anywhere, I want to stay here."

"You are here to teach," the voice responded back.

The light went out and Dan thought, "What the hell just happened?"[222] Now one could make the argument that perhaps Dan had indeed fallen asleep given his exhaustion following the day's events at Gen Con. Coupled with the group discussion of aliens still fresh in his mind, this could have influenced his thought patterns to produce such a vivid dream. But Dan says he never remembers actually falling asleep and insists that he was still conscious during this event. When Dan "came to," he found himself on his back with the covers neatly and tightly tucked across his chest, although he says he never sleeps on his back, he always sleeps on his stomach.

In a few alien abduction reports, the abductee might wake up to find themselves in a similar manner. The bed sheets could be tucked tightly

221 Doty, Dan. Phone interview. 22 March 2017.

222 Doty, Dan. Phone interview. 22 March 2017.

around them, sometimes so tight that they won't even be able to move, giving new meaning to the term "sleep tight" as abductees like Michelle LaVigne describe.[223] But Dan doesn't consider himself to be an abductee when I asked him about this possibility. He had certainly thought about it before, but based on his experiences, he doesn't think that is the case.

Something Dan told me later on was that following his final Bigfoot encounter he developed an acute ability to see people's auras. This ability remained with him, occurring on and off from 1987 through 1997, yet it seemed to disappear after this incident with the ring of light at Gen Con. This was something he actually enjoyed being able to do and was quite upset when it was presumably absent.

Another thing that stood out to me was how Dan did not make a big deal of the event following the incident and did not mention it to his friends whatsoever. Could he have still been in shock over the encounter? His friends certainly observed his change of personality the last day of the convention, as he didn't seem very talkative or active apart from buying a movie script from one of the vendors. In fact, Dan says he was not trying to think about the incident, which he also thought was odd, given his fascination with the paranormal. "It's very gestalt. Like it *was*. That's it," he described it rather cryptically.[224]

There are no accounts of anyone in his family ever having shared with him strange encounters or experiences of their own. In interviewing people and researching various cases, I've found that being a witness to strange phenomenon appears to be a possible family trait for reasons unknown. But here that does not seem to be the case. "If anything happened to them, they never mentioned it. Every time something weird happened to me, I talked about it. I talked about it with everybody and anybody I could find," Dan said.[225]

It wasn't until November of the same year that Dan had another similar otherworldly encounter, this time in his own home. It was about 9:00 am when he had arrived home from working the night shift prior. He was exhausted, so he went to bed immediately. He was abruptly awoken though when he felt like somebody had pushed his head down to prevent him from looking up. At that same time, he felt a presence underneath him

---

223 *Dreamland.* Premiere Radio Networks. 21 Jan. 1996.

224 Doty, Dan. Phone interview. 22 March 2017.

225 Doty, Dan. Phone interview. 22 March 2017.

too. Once he was able to force his head up, he came face-to-face with the stereotypical gray alien.

Dan doesn't believe this event was a dream since he remembers having physically touched the being's shoulder and face. In fact, he described its skin texture as rough, like dry human skin similar to eczema. He also described the being's eyes as not quite as big as most people think of when they envision the classic, solid black alien eyes. "They are still bigger than humans. Maybe twice, maybe three times the size, but not as humongous like we see on the illustrations."[226]

At that point, Dan felt like the entity was now afraid of him because he was no longer under its "control." But it wasn't so much a physical control as it was a mental control, according to his impression. Once he came to that realization he immediately fell back asleep again. He remembers that later on he suddenly "came to," but for only a few minutes, jittery and nervous trying to make sense of what had just taken place. Before he could fully process his emotions he fell back into the sleep state almost immediately again.

When Dan finally mentioned this and the prior event at Gen Con to his friends, they were naturally apprehensive. The most sympathy he received was that they believed that he believed it. So, one night, when two of his friends, Craig and Terry, went outside for a smoke break, Dan decided that perhaps he could somehow prove these entities' existence one and for all to them. As he peered out into the darkness he said quietly, "Okay guys, prove that you're real." But nothing happened. As they were back outside just about to call it a night and head home, Dan says that suddenly out of nowhere a pair of owls in the woods began to make all sorts of commotion and noise.

"Son of a gun, they did it," Dan thought.[227] But could this have been a mere coincidence—a prime example of one man trying to connect two unrelated things together? Dan thinks otherwise and makes reference to another incident, which further supports his rationale.

While in bed on a separate evening, Dan was abruptly overcome with an inexplicable tingly sensation throughout his entire body. He felt like he weighed a ton as he felt himself sinking further into the bed mattress. The event seemingly lasted forever, when in reality it had been just a few seconds. After this sensation had ended, the repetitive sound of an owl

---

226 Doty, Dan. Phone interview. 22 March 2017.

227 Doty, Dan. Phone interview. 22 March 2017.

hooting from the corner of the bedroom began. Dan was certainly aware of owls that lived outside of his house, but none inside the house, which is where the sound had emanated.

It is interesting to note the connection between owls and the paranormal. Owls are thought to be carriers from the spirit realm into the physical world according to Native American philosophy. They also have a strong connection to alien abductees who identify with them for whatever reason. Researcher Mike Clelland has uncovered plenty of reports, which also seem to suggest this as chronicled in his book, *The Messengers: Owls, Synchronicity and the UFO Abductee.* Other abduction researchers speculate on the legitimacy in certain memories that abductees recall, especially when animals appear just before or after an abduction event. It has been suggested that these recollections of animal encounters are actually screen memories used to mask the notion that the animals were really the visitors themselves.

Dawn DeVito, the woman I mentioned earlier who had a series of strange encounters, also possesses an irrational and intense fear of owls, but was unaware of the owl-abductee connection when she told me about it. She too has had ongoing experiences, which possibly suggest an abduction-type scenario. Dan Doty also had no knowledge of the owl connection when he relayed to me his experiences. Furthermore, he stated, "I've always connected the guys upstairs with owls. I don't know why, but it's just the way it is."[228]

Events in Dan's life had reached a lull until one afternoon in the late summer of 2004. He had stepped outside of the local library for a cigarette break when he noticed two white objects in the sky that loomed overhead like plastic bags. At first, they appeared like bags next to a large electrical tower, yet upon closer inspection he noticed the objects maneuvered completely unlike plastic bags. As the objects circled the tower, a tiny, extremely-low-altitude cloud (approximately 100 feet from the ground) entered the objects' vicinity. It traveled against the direction of the wind and abruptly stopped. One of the white objects broke off from its circular trajectory and shot up a straight path into the cloud. The cloud then reversed back in the direction from which it came.

The second white object stopped its motion and made a beeline straight for Dan. Before it would have hit him however, the object made a sharp left, accelerated back into the sky and disappeared from view. When

228 Doty, Dan. Phone interview. 22 March 2017.

the object had been just above his head for a brief moment, Dan saw its structure, which he said clearly wasn't a plastic bag, but rather resembled "a blood cell in its natural form."[229]

Sometimes after conversing with people about their encounters with the strange, the strange seems to leave a sort of echo effect. After I phoned Dan for the first time, events took place that neither him nor I had expected, which is rather fitting given the unexpected nature of the phenomenon itself. The next day, he received a visit to his home in Missouri from two Mormon missionaries. In their conversation, he had referenced something about his past—an obscure Midwestern drive-in restaurant from childhood known as *Dog n' Suds*. Immediately upon ending his discussion, he closed the door behind him and received a notification on his phone. It alerted him to a recommendation email from Amazon for a line of root beer—distributed by who else, but the very same Dog n' Suds brand Dan had just referenced.

Meanwhile, back in Philly, I had opened up the file to begin writing the very chapter you are now reading, when I received a phone call from a number I didn't recognize. At first glance I thought it was peculiar given that it was eerily similar to my own number in the first six digits—but the last four digits were completely different. A similar telemarketing technique has been in place for several years now that takes advantage of spoofing somebody's full number, according to an article from *CNBC.*[230] The report speculated that if telemarketers catch the recipient's curiosity whenever they see their own number displayed on the Caller ID, there is a greater chance they will actually want to answer the call, instead of ignoring it.

I picked up, but as soon as I said "hello," the caller immediately hung up. Since I'm no stranger to the various telemarketing tactics out there, I like to research a phony offender, acquire that company's name, and then report them to the FTC's Do Not Call Registry, which I am quite fond of, along with plenty other Americans fed up with the endless schemes. But when the search results revealed that the number was connected not to a company, but rather to an individual by the name of Paul Doty, I was rather surprised. I found this to be quite odd given that I had just spoken with

229 Doty, Dan. Phone interview. 22 March 2017.

230 Weisbaum, Herb. "Hello, it's me: ID spoofers' latest tactic is a doozy." *CNBC.* NBCUniversal. 16 July 2014. Web. 23 Sept. 2017. https://www.cnbc.com/2014/07/16/hello-its-me-id-spoofers-latest-tactic-is-a-doozy.html

Dan Doty the night before and how he used to receive hang-up calls to his landline for a number of years whenever he picked up.

You bet I called that number back! But instead of hearing a voice on the other line, I was directed straight to an automated voicemail greeting devoid of any sort of personalized introduction. Drat. I had hoped for a mechanical MIB voice instead.

I decided to take a step further with an internet search on the name "Paul Doty." The name belonged to a deceased professor of biochemistry at Harvard who had worked on the Manhattan Project as a graduate student. Later on, this same professor provided the laboratory where the reverse hybridization of DNA was discovered. This holds little meaning until you factor in that the hybridization of DNA (from an alien abduction viewpoint) was the very last thing Dan and I talked about in our phone conversation. Not to mention that the year 1947 (when the Manhattan Project ended) is also regarded as the informal birth year of modern ufology.

A number of people receive these same types of hang-up calls on a weekly basis. But if this really is a telemarketing ploy, then why are telemarketers simply just disconnecting the call once the person picks up? Isn't the whole point of telemarketing to try and get somebody to answer so that they can be sold on a new product or service? Plus, I still haven't heard of telemarketers who now listen in on conversations between two people the night before. Only the government does that, I thought.

On a lighter note, Dan called attention to the fact that the digits in the phone number that called me add up to the number 42. This is the answer that Google returns with if a search is performed for "the answer to life, the universe and everything." The search return is a tribute to Douglas Adams' classic novel, *The Hitchhiker's Guide to the Galaxy.*

In that story, a group of highly intelligent, dimensional beings demand to learn the answer to the ultimate question of life, the universe and everything from a supercomputer named Deep Thought, specially built for the purpose of disseminating information—a forerunner to the internet if you consider its application. It takes Deep Thought 7.5 million years to compute and check on the answer, which turns out to be 42.

I guess the spectrum can have a sense of humor about itself too.

"On one hand I want to tell everybody, I want to scream it from the highest mountaintops. On the other hand, it's profoundly embarrassing, and I sound like an idiot."[231]

– David M. Jacobs, PhD.

231 *Coast to Coast AM*. Premiere Radio Networks, 20 Oct. 2015.

Final Thoughts

Since I began work on this book, peculiar events have taken place, which led me to suspect that the subject matter I wrote about somehow influenced these things to hone in on me. Perhaps I gave off a mental beacon whenever I explored the independent components of the experience that somehow attracted these forces. Or maybe it was all just wishful thinking on my part that somehow grew to manifest and become a self-fulfilling prophecy in the end.

We should always keep a healthy perspective in our experiences instead of immediately assuming that the spectrum of strange phenomena is to blame. As evident in the events that involved several of my friends receiving bizarre phone calls, anything could have been responsible for it, really—from general telecommunication glitches, to telemarketers, to obsessive exes using call spoofing programs.

The following day, after completing the first draft of this book, I received a knock on my front door from two uniformed police officers. Since I wasn't home at the time I'll never know for sure, but I assume the two men just had the wrong address. They left as quickly as they had arrived, according to my neighbor. Yet to wishful thinkers, this would be a sure sign of the Men in Black, contrary to the men in blue without an accurate GPS. In reality, the MIB scenario is probably the furthest thing from the truth. Or at least I hope so, in my case.

When we (the ones actively looking into high strangeness) become so saturated in the subject, we tend to become obsessed with it. It's acceptable and reasonably expected for those of us in this field to take a break every now and again to focus on other more human things to do with our lives. This, of course, is to project a more sane impression of ourselves that our friends and families will be quite thankful for. And also to protect ourselves—not just from a one-way ticket to the loony bin, but also from the forces within the spectrum that seek to drive us crazy at every turn.

It could be our mindsets which inadvertently send out beacons that these forces sooner or later hone in on. Perhaps that is why those that tend to have a more perceptive ability, or a greater awareness overall, quickly find themselves as easy targets for the phenomena. I've provided plenty of examples of such for you to ponder, at the very least.

John Keel noted that investigators tend to concentrate on the very subjective descriptions of the observers while he himself often dug deeper to study the witnesses themselves. Keel was able to find that many of the witnesses suffered from such ailments as temporary amnesia, intense headaches, muscle spasms, excessive thirst and other effects similar to those seen in religious miracles, demonology, occult phenomena, and even contacts with fairies. He believed that as a result, these things all shared a common source or cause.[232]

Another challenging aspect for investigators to deal with is found in an otherwise saturated field of thrill-seekers and troublemakers. Much to the surprise of those that get into it just to make a buck or two, there's hardly any significant profit to be made. Those that have had limited financial success worked their butts off and left behind a trail of dust, debris and the occasional shell of where their former *normal* selves used to be. Whether or not it's worth a single penny in the end, there's no doubt this pursuit changes an individual for better, or for worse.

Then there's the never-ending appetite for the unsolvable and the unreachable, which somehow connects it (and us) together in one way or another. It forever feeds a void that exists within the soul. *There must be something else out there beyond this!*

Biblical scholars speculate that once we attain union with God after departure from this realm, we get to spend the rest of eternity learning about and discovering all that He possesses. If that's so, then it might make more sense how we never seem to be any closer to solving the UFO enigma or making the case for ghosts than we were a hundred, if not a thousand years ago. Technology isn't going to bring us any closer and neither will the science community, should they ever choose to accept this as science fact.

---

232 Keel, John A. *The Mothman Prophecies.* 1975. New York: Tor Books, 2002. pg. 43.

To the dismay of my colleagues, the subject may simply be one of those avenues of fringe research that will always remain a mystery for as long as humans are present on this planet. Why? Because we're simply not meant to fully comprehend it...

...at least not yet.

But as much as I try to pull myself out of the topic, I find myself pulled right back in. There are times when I need to distance myself from all the weirdness, but my vacation is rather short-lived. The elusive has a peculiar fondness to keep us engaged. It seems to enjoy keeping us within its reach, yet also keeping us at bay. It loves to tap at our door, yet hide as soon as we open it. It whispers in our ears, yet turns away when we turn towards it. I have little hope that we'll ever truly receive all the answers we seek, simply because it doesn't seem to have any interest in ever revealing itself to us fully or completely.

In Ingo Swann's experiences in the 1970s, he dealt with a shadowy figurehead named "Axelrod." Ingo brought up not being able to initially recall those extraordinary paranormal (and paranoid-filled) encounters he had at that time. He wrestled with the notion that somehow the turn of events with Axelrod ought to be indelibly etched into his memory somehow, and yet surprisingly, it wasn't. This puzzled him to such an extent that Ingo began to wonder if there wasn't something associated with the events themselves that had somehow been connected to a sort of amnesia which took time to bring back up to the surface.[233]

Ingo wondered if people in general aren't really caught up in some kind of strange, but collective amnesia that is somehow unknowingly induced as a result of these experiences. It reminded him of a science-fiction synopsis dealing with social-wide amnesia having to do with hypnotic commands to FORGET what we have seen and ATTACK and DESTROY those who insist they've seen it.[234]

Are these same forces that we cannot see, and may not even be aware of in some instances, subtly influencing us? The Apostle Paul wrote that

---

233 Swann, Ingo. "UFOs Everywhere-Denials Everywhere, Too." *Penetration: The Question of Extraterrestrial and Human Telepathy.* Kindle ed., Panta Rei/Crossroad Press, 2014. Location 1272.

234 Swann, Ingo. "UFOs Everywhere-Denials Everywhere, Too." *Penetration: The Question of Extraterrestrial and Human Telepathy.* Kindle ed., Panta Rei/Crossroad Press, 2014. Location 1316.

our true battles are not in the physical realm, but rather against the sight unseen.[235] So we should always be on guard and aware of such things, even if our intentions are believed to be coming from a higher place. For even those things may not appear as they seem, either. Angels of darkness can also masquerade as angels of light,[236] so we need to be more discerning overall. Just because the so-called "space brothers" tell contactees that they're here to raise humanity's awareness or save planet Earth from death and destruction doesn't mean we should necessarily believe them at face value.

It's easy to jump on the bandwagon and conclude that the major governments of the world, or more specifically, the United States government, is keeping the lid on this phenomenon, its visitors, and the forces associated with it. People are quick to conclude that there's a vast conspiracy fueled by a desire to hold power over people and keep control of the populations of the world. It would be easy to assume that there is also this vast free energy conspiracy in existence in order to keep the oil conglomerates operating throughout the world, feeding our massive consumption of natural resources. There could be a shadowy elite that exists behind the scenes and possesses all the secrets. The list of what-ifs goes on longer than a child's letter to Santa.

But what if maybe, just *maybe,* the cover-up is for our own good? Insert the collective groans from all the believers now...

Let's consider two main parts behind such a theory—the acceptance and the allowance. Accepting or acknowledging the phenomenon might allow such a doorway to be opened, similar to when we become tuned-in to the phenomenon, from which there is no turning back. Once these things have been allowed to enter into our reality, there's no telling where that will lead. Keel noted in his research that the phenomenon is dependent on belief. And as more people buy into the concept that occupants of gravity-defying ships are from the stars, then the real forces behind them can manipulate more of us through false illumination. He was worried that this unchecked "disease" of the UFO belief would eventually lead to a new faith in the extraterrestrials and allow them to interfere explicitly in our affairs.[237]

---

235 *The Bible.* Ephesians 6:12, New International Version, Biblica, 1973, 1978, 1984, 2011.

236 *The Bible.* 2 Corinthians 11:13-15, New International Version, Biblica, 1973, 1978, 1984, 2011.

237 Keel, John A. *The Mothman Prophecies.* 1975. New York: Tor Books, 2002. pg. 168.

So, what if the part of the government's stance on this all along was to downplay, discredit, debunk and ridicule in order to protect us from being controlled by such a phenomenon? Perhaps if the government did reveal to the public the truth about the phenomenon, that these forces within the spectrum do indeed exist (i.e, disclosure), it would allow them to enter into our own reality full-time, all the time? Psychic-mediums often make mention of "closing a door" to keep such unwanted entities out of our world, so what if there was actually something to that concept, but on a much larger scale?

When I consider the experiences of so many people in this book and beyond, I find that they are important not just because of their content, but because they are of several examples that span the spectrum of strange phenomena. We can learn from each of them in their commonalities, as well as their differences. Yet in the pursuit of the subject of high strangeness in general, one niche is often kept separate from another, even if the descriptions of the experiences overlap into the many different genres and subgenres.

For example, the nuts-and-bolts UFO investigators don't like to get into the aspects of metaphysical or paranormal implications, as much as the Bigfoot guys tend to exclude the connection to UFOs in their reports. Or how ghost hunters are confused to hear deceased relatives showing up in the midst of an alien abduction, as much as psychics discount temporary telepathic abilities in those who have had such close encounters. Why do we have to keep the niches separated when there is clear overlap between them?

Perhaps in our own rudimentary logic we can't explain the phenomena in the way we had hoped, so this is the best we can do just to maintain some sort of control. At least it is some sort of organizational system, flawed and incomplete, as it may be. But it's this isolation in each category or subcategory, which keeps the spectrum from being examined on a larger scope to identify similarities and commonalities within each of its forms.

It's like when government subcontracts use compartmentalization techniques to keep individual contributors from learning what others are working on. It's a common practice to keep all the other cogs in the wheel left in the dark so the individual cogs can't complete the bigger picture to see they are part of a larger, more impactful project.

If we could just set aside our preconceived notions of what we *think* the phenomena is, compared to what it really is, then maybe what it actually is will start to become a little less foggy and convoluted. Then we might be able to gain clarity into those bigger questions we're always in search of.

The phenomena within the spectrum is forever changing and evolving. It doesn't fit into the typical mold of what we've often come to expect. These inexplicable realms, beings and forces have always existed throughout human history. We just have a tendency to label them and re-label them to reflect our cultural views and societal belief systems at the time.

That being said, I wonder what the monsters, phantoms, flying ships and their occupants will take the form of one hundred years from now. Let's hope it's just as interesting and engaging as the human experience as a whole—the biggest mystery of all.

About the Author

Justin Bamforth has been exploring paranormal phenomena, the UFO topic, and other areas of high strangeness for close to twenty years. He lectures on the subject, collaborates with researchers on cases, and consults with people across the globe to better understand whatever it is we're dealing with. Or at least he attempts to.

Justin holds two degrees, one in Graphic Design and another in Digital Arts, where he spends most of his nine-to-five in advertising and marketing—an equally bizarre world of its own.

He currently resides in the Philadelphia metro area and can usually be found with either a cat on his lap, a cup of hot tea in hand, or good music in his ears. Justin also pens screenplays and song lyrics in addition to poetry, blogging, copywriting, and numerous other time-wasting endeavors.

The author can be reached at...

NormalParanormal.org

JustinBamforth.com

Made in the USA
Columbia, SC
04 April 2019